Broken ~~Hill~~

The Broken Road to Becoming Whole:
A Journey of Transformation

Fiona Demark

First published by Ultimate World Publishing 2024
Copyright © 2024 Fiona Demark

ISBN

Paperback: 978-1-923123-86-1
Ebook: 978-1-923123-87-8

Fiona Demark has asserted her rights under the Copyright, Designs and Patents Act 1988 to be identified as the author of this work. The information in this book is based on the author's experiences and opinions. The publisher specifically disclaims responsibility for any adverse consequences which may result from use of the information contained herein. Permission to use information has been sought by the author. Any breaches will be rectified in further editions of the book.

All rights reserved. No part of this publication may be reproduced, stored in or introduced into a retrieval system, or transmitted in any form, or by any means (electronic, mechanical, photocopying, recording or otherwise) without the prior written permission of the author. Any person who does any unauthorised act in relation to this publication may be liable to criminal prosecution and civil claims for damages. Enquiries should be made through the publisher.

Cover design: Ultimate World Publishing
Layout and typesetting: Ultimate World Publishing
Editor: Alex Floyd-Douglass
Cover Image Copyright: Jason Benz Bennee-Shutterstock.com

Ultimate World Publishing
Diamond Creek,
Victoria Australia 3089
www.writeabook.com.au

Acknowledgements

Thanks to my Dad for the gift of resilience, my sisters for their demonstrated persistence and the friends who believed in me when I did not believe in myself.

To my mother, for giving me life, despite the relationship challenges that came to be.

To Garry Mason, who wasn't afraid to ask the tough questions and hear the answers. And to the Godress family who took me under their wings, into their home and into their hearts, providing opportunities upon which I could dream of a future.

And to all the bullies and naysayers who made the journey difficult, I also acknowledge you – for without those challenges, I would not be the woman I am today.

Introduction

This book is written from my memories and I possibly have taken some creative license – especially with dialogue – as my memory is far from photographic. How I experienced events may be nothing like how others remember them. That is the interesting thing about our brains; we select what we wish to remember and the interpretation that comes with it.

There are some really tough times that I reflect upon during these pages. Here, I offer a **trigger warning** for suicide and other traumas I experienced during these years. For me, they are things in the past that I have lived through and come to terms with. I hope that reading these pages will give you some insight into what it was like for a girl with a disability growing up in a place that offered difficult circumstances – not only with the management of my vision loss but in the other encounters that life brought my way.

Relationships with others play an important role in the story of these years. I know that without the support I had from the people who offered it, this story would be a very different one. Sometimes, people are in our lives for a reason, and those moments may be fleeting or long-term. Everyone I mention in these pages was integral to my navigation through the years described.

When I left Broken Hill, I had the opportunity to reinvent myself. I could start from scratch and be the person I wanted people to know, not the person with assumptions made about them and was judged on the whims of the school bully and the latest rumour or nasty taunt that went around school.

Some may be surprised at the things I speak about in these pages; I have tried to be as open and honest as possible, often typing with tears in my eyes, both for the happy and sad moments. I share with an open heart and for those of you who know me personally and read this, I hope you have some deeper insight into the person I am today because of the stories I share from my younger years.

Flames and Fire

The bitter chill of a winter night gave me more than chills down my spine from the cold; it was the night that was the catalyst for my life to change forever. It was the night of the 4th of June 1989. It was not only the night that my earthly possessions were all lost but also my father's sixty-eighth birthday. What would prevail was an unexpected and devastating birthday gift for him and a crushing blow that echoed through every corner of our small family.

A surprise birthday party was organised at a family friend's house. My father was not one much for surprises – nor parties for that matter – so us having plans for his birthday was unusual. I remember getting all prissied up thinking I was going to some Hollywood party as you do when you are a twelve-year-old girl and *Dolly* magazine shows you your life goals.

I was far from your average teenager but far from the level of maturity that night was to bring forth. Spending so much time and attention on my clothing selection and presentation, I danced around my bedroom, listening and singing along to my favourite tunes pumping out of the portable cassette player. A moment of true self-indulgent bliss – the calm before the storm.

As we prepared to leave the house, I patted my cat Peppy – who was sleeping on the end of my bed – and told him to be a good cat and stay warm. As we drove up the road from the house, I distinctly recall turning back and glancing towards the front light we had left on and said, "Goodbye, house."

It seems an extraordinary thing to do on reflection, but maybe subconsciously, I knew something was wrong. It was not an action I had ever done before, and I noted it was strange as I did it; perhaps it was a premonition of the disaster ahead.

The surprise birthday party was held in the warmth of a friend's house, with around twenty of our closest family and friends in attendance. With the cake cut and the candles all blown out, the party was beginning to wind down. Little did we know there was a more ominous fire, not to be put out so quickly, burning away on the other side of town.

The jovial atmosphere was abruptly shattered by a frantic knocking at the front door of the house we were visiting. In a small town, it takes little time to track down where a person is at any given moment. I remember the person who came to the door asking the homeowner if my parents were there and to request them to attend right away as their house was burning down.

In the panic that ensued, my parents, gripped by fear, rushed to the scene, leaving me behind, perhaps to shield me from the harsh reality. For in their eyes, I was still a child.

What seemed like hours crept by. I helped tidy up after all the party guests left and the family and friends did their best to distract me from thinking, worrying and assuming the worst. In those desperate times of waiting, the brain can create all sorts of scenarios – often none quite right and often more catastrophic than reality. In this case, however, the facts surpassed my imagination.

The return of my parents bore the stench of smoke. It clung to their clothes and hair, and they had ash marks on their skin and clothing. They looked exhausted.

I imagine they were still in shock from witnessing something so terrible. The realisation hit that we had nothing and nowhere to go. Our home had been reduced to ashes. It was time for bed, but I had no bed to sleep in. We stayed the night with my half-sister and her family.

Being the eldest of my siblings, and the only one still residing in town, it seemed only normal for her to offer the place to seek refuge. The enormity of the situation hit me when she gave me a t-shirt to sleep in. I had no clothes of my own – except my party outfit I had dedicated so much attention to choosing only hours before.

Perched at the end of a street on the outskirts of town with a quarry as one neighbour and a vacant block as another, our house had been a solitary dwelling with several sheds and other outbuildings on the property. Built in a typical style for the town at the time: a wood structure with a corrugated iron outer, the house had no chance against the ferocity of the fire.

A night worker at the quarry had raised the alarm. He heard a loud explosion and looked over towards a roaring fire. Estimating the location, he called the fire service to attend. When the emergency services arrived, the house was alight with flames at the front and the firefighters entered by breaking the back door. As they did, they noticed a little tabby cat run out and off into the yard but were focused on establishing if anyone was in the house and putting the fire out.

The neighbour from across the vacant block advised that the house's residents had gone out for the night and, therefore, the firefighters could focus on putting out the fire. The house was already destroyed, but the focus was ensuring the flames did not reach the adjacent outbuildings and the bushland surrounding the house at the back.

The following morning, I returned with my parents to the remains of the house. My parents were escorted through the charred ruin by the firefighters, but I was kept at the property edge. Again, a reflection upon the fact that I was only a child and had no place amongst the devastation. The part of the house that contained my parents' bedroom and the living room had been completely destroyed, with the following two rooms behind experiencing severe damage. The back of the house where my bedroom was located had not burned but had been affected by smoke and water and had some structural damage.

I was stuck in a moment, standing, feeling helpless, listening to everyone around me and knowing that this was no longer my home. In fact, I had no home, no possessions, and was feeling a profound sense of loss.

The most poignant memory is that of the smell. It is unique to a house fire and is the combined smell of smoke from the structure burning and the fumes expelled from the contents of the house as they burned. The smoke permeated every part of me. It stayed on our clothes, in our hair, everywhere I went. For months afterwards, it seemed like that smell of smoke followed me.

The local press attended and captured the aftermath, freezing our moment of despair for the newspaper's front-page story the following day. Here we all were, wearing yesterday's clothing and borrowed things. It was icy, with the wind blowing and the acrid smell of burnt house everywhere. It seemed as though everyone was doing something around me, and my world just stopped.

I felt truly alone and scared and, for the first time, realised that the things I considered necessary were unimportant. Who cared if the kids at school were a bit mean or my friend did not want to talk to me for some teenage girl slight? This was big, and it would not be big just for now, but it would affect the rest of my life.

I was broken from my moment of reflection by my dad approaching. He had something hidden in the jacket he was wearing. He grabbed my hand and said, *"I have something for you."*

He then reached under the coat and brought out a terrified but very much alive little tabby cat.

"Peppy!" I grabbed my poor little kitty and hugged him so hard. I cried like a baby and promised I would never let him go. The firefighter who had broken the door down the night before came over to me and told me that he had seen the cat run out of the door as they entered the house and had gone to look for him in

the yard while the supervisor was walking my parents through the ruin. He found him in the shed and took my dad to fetch him from his hiding spot. That little kitty used up more than one of his nine lives that night, and I was so glad to have him in my arms to hug.

The cause of the fire was attributed to old and faulty wiring in the electrical system, with the explosion that the night worker heard being the shorting out of the power fuse box. Later, we found fuses ejected from the fuse box on the other side of the road from our property, so the explosion must have been very fierce. Part of the devastation from a residential house fire is the toxic gas released by household furnishings.

Quite often, this is the leading cause of the poisonous smoke inhalation that people experience and what gives a house fire a distinct smell like no other. In the instance of what happened at my house, something must have been on a slow burn that caused these toxins to start their release, even before the main explosion from the electrical system.

My parents also both owned a cat. Abbey, my mother's cat, was sleeping on my parent's bed; this is where they found her curled-up little body when they walked through the house. My Dad's cat, Boofus, was found sleeping forever on his chair in the kitchen. Only because I had the back bedroom, and that is no doubt where my little Peppy kitty was when the fire started, this enabled him to escape. How sad that the pets did not even have a chance to wake up and save themselves; however, maybe suffocating from toxic smoke when you are asleep is better than burning to death, which is what may have happened had they been awake and tried to escape.

The demise of Abbey and Boofus was a true example of how much more devastating this fire could have been. On a Sunday night in winter, it would not have been unusual for the family to have been in bed by around 9pm, which is when the fire was expected to have started. My father was an early riser, early-to-bed kind of guy, and my mother had not been feeling all that well that day, so no doubt, would have been in bed too. Even if I were still awake, my bedroom – situated at the back of the house – was not close to where the fire broke out, and so by the time I had been alerted, my ability to do anything practical would have been limited.

From what the fire crew could discern from the evidence, the fire had started in or near my parents' room. Being asleep at the time, they would most likely have suffered the same fate as the cats and would have died from inhaling the toxins from the smoke.

Now, I know that we were all lucky to be alive, or at a minimum, I'm fortunate that I am not an orphan. Okay, that's a plus. And I had my kitty. That's another plus. But I literally had nothing else. Not even a change of undies or a toothbrush. We were told by the fire service that the site would be signed off for the insurance investigator to attend, and they all left. The press departed, and my parents and I were left to stand looking at the ruin of our house.

For me, the years of my life with all my memories and things I had collected along the way. For my parents, their last sixteen years of living in that house and a lifetime of collected keepsakes, trinkets and memorabilia all lost. For household items like televisions or clothes, you can go out and buy new ones. It's the things that are irreplaceable: photographs, personal momentous, the family christening dress, or the gifts my grandmother had passed down before she died; all of those things are irreplaceable. And, of course, my parents were also grieving their little furry friends that didn't make it.

We returned to my half-sister's house, which became our headquarters for the next few weeks. Little did she know when she offered us a place to stay that it meant everyone would be passing through her home.

The insurance agency's assessors came to interview my parents and assess the ruin. The house was a total loss, with the remnants needing to be bulldozed. The site was cleared for us to salvage any items from the destruction that we could and signed off on. But as these things do, the payout took some time. A family friend transferred some cash to my parent's bank to enable them to purchase the essentials. As mentioned, we did not have clean underwear or toiletries, and these funds allowed us to buy such necessities. My parents did not even have a bank book to use at the bank to withdraw savings. I remember my mother retelling the story of the argument she had with the bank teller in relation to her incapacity to provide the relevant identification. This is just a small example of a seemingly everyday task that had been complicated by the events of the house fire.

Literally, everything had gone up in smoke.

The community spirit in a country town comes to the forefront in times such as these. I remember offerings from community-based charity groups and individuals who knew of our plight from our story in the newspaper. We had endless donations dropped off at my half-sister's house. Blankets, clothing, and other household essentials. I recall someone even brought some cat food for Peppy. The living and dining room looked like a charity store with items packed everywhere. It's heart-warming when you are at the end of a community's generosity and giving spirit. As kind and thoughtful as all of this was, the personal things I had lost still had the most impact.

I have always been a great fan of music, and as of my previous birthday, I was gifted my first cassette player and tapes with my own music tastes. This differed from the type donated, and I felt lost without music. Music was and is my escape, so the opportunity to withdraw from reality was taken away. My other escape was books and reading.

Of course, my books were all smoky and water-damaged from the fire. This was something, however, that was donated. I remember for the week or so after the fire; I would find a quiet corner and a book in one of the donation boxes and escape from the reality of my situation into fiction and fantasy. I would do this many times over the coming months as a coping mechanism and a way to remove myself from what was going on around me.

A week after the house fire, it was time to return to school. It was my first year of high school. As it was a small town and I had been absent from school for a week, it was common knowledge what had happened to my family and our house.

Dad took me to the school office on my first day back. The staff took me to the lost property and donations bin for the uniforms and found me a couple of school jumpers that would fit and a donated winter skirt. The winter uniform had recently changed, so only a few choices existed. I recollect having to choose a shirt that was a size too big. I could piece together enough to meet uniform regulations, and then came the task to replace all my books and texts.

I was given a student pack with stationery and exercise books to put my work in. Then, I had to visit all the departments and speak to the head teacher to be issued another copy of the subject textbooks to replace the ones damaged in the fire. It felt as though everyone was so kind but overwhelmingly so, to the point where I was just ready to go back into my corner at home – well not at home because I did not have one – at our borrowed home and escape again. The reality of this situation was just too much and having to retell the story over and over again was exhausting. I had not seen any other students yet but dealing with the staff had been an ordeal.

I packed my hand-me-down backpack with my new books and headed to school the following day. I arrived to find my friends, whom I had not seen or spoken to for the week since the fire happened. They were full of questions, of which I had no energy to answer as once you tell the same story many times, you simply repeat yourself and then remind yourself of the thing you want most to forget.

Teenagers are curious creatures, though, and of course, my friends wanted to know the story so they could support me – not simply for juicy gossip, which was not the case with many others from the student body. Even though it was common knowledge that I had lost everything, I was teased about my poorly fitting uniform and lack of school items.

For some, borrowing classmates' books and rewriting six months of notes would be a huge chore; I saw it as a chance for revision and another distraction from everything happening around me. It's funny how it was so difficult for teachers to locate the handouts from classes they taught months ago. There were still gaps in the course content that I could never replace.

I missed the original workbooks. The ones I had painstakingly covered in book wraps colour-coded for each subject and then covered in clear contact to protect them. Note to self: clear contact will protect a book from getting damaged in a school bag or can be wiped if you put it on a dirty surface; it will not help it withstand the smoke from a fire or the water from a fire hose.

In the generosity that comes from country folk, a family offered us a house to live in as a temporary measure while the insurance claim was being processed and my parents located a new home to buy. Dad had helped the family – who were currently living in the residence over the corner shop they ran – to renovate their house, ready to move into when they retired at the end of the year. As my father had single-handedly renovated most of the inside of their home and they were not using it, it was offered to my parents at no charge while we got back on our feet.

This house was not a real home or a place to call my own, but it was much better than sharing a room with my nephew. I at least had a room and could start rebuilding my life. At twelve, a girl needs her privacy and a place to escape to. I had commandeered a big, blue, fluffy blanket that had been donated and spent many hours draped in that blanket in my borrowed bedroom reading and doing my homework. Peppy often curled up with me. It became a temporary sanctuary where I could escape from the reality of what was going on around me, for short periods of time.

Finally, my parents were given the all-clear to salvage the contents of the house ruin before the remains were destroyed. To this day, it amazes me the things we managed to recover. Some photographs had been in a metal cake tin on a shelf that could be salvaged, and a photo album that – although it had been damaged – most of the photos inside could be removed and retained.

The fire had destroyed most of what was in the front rooms, and little could be retrieved from there. The dining area had all the fancy dinnerware, which mainly had smoke damage, so there were crystal glass vases and serving plates of different kinds that could be taken out of the remnants of the dining buffet and taken away for cleaning.

Everything had that awful black smoke smell on it and needed to be soaked in the laundry basin for a day or two and scrubbed clean. I remember this job seemed endless. The whole house smelled like smoke – even the things you thought would not hold a smell did. Some items needed to be cleaned and scrubbed with a toothbrush to get into all the tiny crevices to remove the smoke damage.

Looking back now, as much as I hated this chore, I would do the same. It was almost cathartic to retrieve the things you could and cling to what could be salvaged. Anything that could be cleaned or recovered, we did it. To this day, some family photos have black smoke marks on the edges, and believe it or not, they still have the smoke smell after all this time. But we have those items that I can now pass on to my children one day. Those small trinkets that hold parts of our family history.

Our family dogs, who were in the backyard at the time of the fire, were both unharmed. They remained at the property for the time that it took to remove all the items that could be salvaged before we moved them to our new home. It was the joint responsibility of our German Shepherd and my little black dog to guard the ruin and prevent people from looting the property before it was bulldozed. Imagine the heartache of my father, who attended that property every day to care for the dogs. It must have been such a weight on his heart to see the destroyed house and have the constant reminder of all that was lost.

My parents found a suitable house about three months after we moved to the temporary home. They bought it and told me one afternoon when I was picked up from school. I had never been included in deciding where I would like to live or the new house. I must admit, though, it was not a bad choice, and as I grew up as a teenager, I realised that this location was much better than the previous house for building the independence that I required as a teen and also being able to feel comfortable inviting friends to visit as I got older and was granted more leniency with rules pertaining to visiting friends.

I was allowed to choose the paint colour and carpet for my bedroom and even had a choice as to which room I wanted. Our donated furniture was installed, and I brought the possessions I had accumulated from the house we had been staying in. I was so happy to have my own room and to show Peppy and tell him this was his new home, and he did not need to be afraid anymore of being in strange places. I could put posters on my walls and change the layout of my room as often as I wanted. Having that space of my own, a safe place to hide in when the outside world became too much, a place to be myself, to keep my secrets and to let my guard down was a gift. A teenage girl's bedroom is so much more than a place to sleep. Now, again, I had my own retreat.

My parents and I made a trip to Mildura, a small city 300 kilometres away, and purchased all the items that a family needs which are not donated. A washer and dryer, microwave, and vacuum cleaner and a fridge. All the more minor things like a new kettle and toaster and, most happily for me, a new cassette player. My parents were not willing to spend their insurance payment on a new music collection for me. However, I was allowed to pick two new cassettes and a box of blank cassettes.

I then asked my friends to make copies of their music for me. I remember my Christmas gift that year from my middle sister at university was a box of copied cassettes that were the current charting music she had made from her and her friends' collections. What a thoughtful gift, something that I was genuinely grateful for. I was so happy to have my music back again.

That trip to Mildura, where we could attend the local white goods store along with *Target and Kmart*, felt like such an adventure. Looking back, I realise that my parents would have had to have made a specific list of things they required and then stuck to it. This must have been the first time ever in my parent's life that they had been given such a large amount of money to spend, and it would have been so easy to just blow it on things that were not useful. We used the few months between the fire and this trip to work out the things we needed most. It was weird when you needed something simple like a cheese grater and found that you did not have one anymore. Every time this happened, we added to the list. As a twelve-year-old, I was most interested in music, books and clothes – not at all practical things that build a working household. I remember being packed like a sardine into the back of the car with all of our new purchases for the three-hour trip home. I did not mind at all as it was exciting to have some new things, rather than all the hand me down items we had been relying upon. Of course, not everything fitted into the family car, so we also had to request a delivery. I loved the smell of all the new appliances, such a contrast to the terrible smoky smell.

It amazes me these days how much I'm complacent about the material things that do not matter and paradoxically, things that I treasure and have memories attached to them are items that I ensure are kept safe. Everything else is part of me in some way but also apart. Our photos are backed up digitally and saved as a copy off-site from our house. We have also offered this service to friends, and we hold digital photo albums for several other families.

I have since learned the importance of using the lovely things we have. So often, you see people with fancy dinnerware stashed in the cupboard and they only bring it out for a special occasion. What meets the requirements for the special occasion I am not sure – maybe a visit from royalty – but for us, because I know that all the fancy stuff my parents owned never got used and then mostly was destroyed, I understand the importance of using the items regularly. If I worked hard and now can afford fancy wine glasses that cost fifty dollars a glass, then for sure, I am going to drink my Friday night glass of wine from that sucker.

We all hold on to our possessions as part of us, but if they are all taken away instantly, other things become important. If we take away all our material items, we are left with memories, moments, and the people we love and spend time with. I was lucky that night that it was only belongings that were taken from me. It could easily have been so much worse with both my parents being taken. I was also incredibly blessed to have my cat survive. I was young enough that honestly, the 'stuff' that I had at the time was pretty insignificant, and even though it felt devastating to lose it all, it could have been a much worse experience in the whole scheme of things.

After the fire, as a child, I missed the comfort of safety and security. I missed my things; I had no favourite teddy bear to hug and cry with. The enormity of the events around the fire made me realise that nothing was forever. I had experienced loss when my grandmother had died a few years before, but logically, everyone had to die, and Grandma was old and sick.

I was not ready for the universe to teach me that, in a moment, everything can change and that catastrophic things can happen.

Something you cannot prepare for and things that only seem to happen in the movies or a book. That fateful night took away my childhood innocence as I knew it. I had already learned some harsh lessons in life about resilience, but that night was the moment when I grew to understand that bad things will happen and sometimes it will take every ounce of energy and strength you have inside to navigate a way through.

As devastating as this event was, it was only the beginning of my teen years. In some ways, I am grateful that my naivety was shattered then, because in the not-so-distant future, I was going to need to rely upon that strength and resilience a whole lot more.

The Obstacles of the Outback

As a child, I would run across the red dirt, flitting from shade patch to shade patch, trying not to burn my feet on the scorching hot ground. Most people who have grown up in Australia can relate to this ritual. The barefoot run across the hot earth was a heightened experience in Broken Hill due to the extreme heat of the summer days – where taking refuge in those shady patches provided a momentary shelter from the heat. As children, outside play – even on the hottest of days – was the norm.

Situated in the vast expanse of Far West New South Wales, Broken Hill, a mining town, exudes a distinct personality of its own. Isolated from any major city by over 500 kilometres, it is very remote, attracting numerous short-term residents and the permanent population who have become hardened to the harsh outback environment.

When I was born, the town population was about 20,000, so it's not a small town; however, as it is so isolated and remote, the environment does not seem to make the way we lived the same as other places of a similar size.

I am the youngest of three daughters born to my working-class parents in the 1970s. At the time of my birth, my eldest sister was about to turn twelve and my middle sister was six and a half. My mother worked part-time at the local animal rescue centre before I was born, and my father was a bartender at the local serviceman's club.

In 1973, my parents bought the family home at the end of a street in the South of Broken Hill. It was a simple house with no modern conveniences that we take for granted today. Hot water was only from a bathroom tap connected to the shower and hot water service. This made washing the dishes even less fun when you had to fetch hot water in a bucket to fill the kitchen sink.

When I was young, we had an outside toilet that was *really* outside. We would have to walk about 30 metres to the toilet before bedtime. Especially in the winter, it was an awful experience. My middle sister and I would hold hands, run as fast as we could to the toilet and then complain that each other was taking too long and we were freezing while waiting.

In the summer, we were always scared we'd come across a brown snake on our way to the toilet. I was so happy when my dad installed an indoor toilet when I was about six. Our house had a huge yard and plenty of room for outside play; the blue metal quarry was next to our home at the end of the dead-end street. When I was young, we would sneak across and play in the huge mounds of gravel rocks. It was a hazardous activity and the quarry stopped it when I was around ten by building a cyclone fence around its perimeter that sided our land.

Strangely, the town is separated by enormous piles of dirt resulting from open-cut mining excavations. The South Broken Hill residents need to drive around the piles of dirt every time they go to the central part of the town. Our house was on the street near the dirt piles and the adjacent mine. As a child, I remember hearing the sirens and the mine blasts that would literally shake the ground. I always wondered if there would be a big explosion one day that blew up the whole area. In my musings as a young child, it seemed possible that the entire town would collapse one day from the mine blasts and fall into one big hole.

The mines and the mineral deposits wielded a profound influence on the way the town operated. When the mining companies started downsizing in the 1990s, the city began to feel the effects of the decline. The social structure of the town was very much based upon if the 'man of the family' worked at the mine and if so, what his role was there. Many of my friends' fathers were made redundant and this was extremely difficult as many men had started working at the mine as soon as they were old enough to leave high school at fifteen or sixteen.

Many of the people I went to high school with who left after Grade Ten also applied for jobs with the local mines as job opportunities were limited – especially if you were unskilled and only had a basic high school education. The reduction in the workforce brought many stressors to families and had serious impacts upon the mental health of those made redundant and unable to locate alternative employment locally.

After I was born and my mother returned to work, it was decided that my father, who was nearly twenty years her senior, would be a stay-at-home dad and she would drive for the local taxi company part-time. It was very unusual for my father to take this option. He was the only male parent doing the school drop-offs and pickups.

Today, stay-at-home fathers are not uncommon, but my father definitely broke tradition when he chose to be the caregiver for our family.

Dad took me for the sign-up for my first day of school. I remember him taking me to the principal's office and them talking about how I may need some extra help in class. The principal seemed scary, but Dad assured me that school would be okay and that I would love it. I got my elephant-shaped name tag and held my dad's hand tight on that first walk to the classroom. Dad left me with my new teacher and, in his usual style, made a funny joke to make me relax and feel that I was safe and that he would be back to collect me from class before I knew it.

I knew right away that I did not fit in. The kids were not mean, but many of them knew each other from pre-school, which I had never attended. I made a few friends, but it seemed that whenever in a large group, I was always an outsider.

Against this arid backdrop, my family faced the additional challenge of navigating disability. By the time my eldest sister had turned one, my mother had realised that she had something medically wrong with her eyesight. After being told by the local doctor that she was simply clumsy, my mother took the opportunity to have a consultation with a visiting eye specialist who she heard was in town. He instantly recognised my sister as having some kind of retinal condition and advised that follow-up was required.

Many years passed of trying to work within the limited resources that Broken Hill offered. Eventually, an ophthalmologist was signed up in Adelaide. Little was known about retinal conditions at this time, and my sister was given several incorrect diagnoses. My middle sister exhibited no signs of any deteriorated eyesight when she was born, so my parents assumed that my elder sister's condition was unique to her.

Little did they know that the particular retinal condition is a recessive genetic disorder and when I was born, as both of my parents carried the gene, I inherited the condition. At least in my situation, my parents had a head start and I was able to be diagnosed quickly and attended the same specialist consultants as my sister.

Despite her low vision, my eldest sister often took responsibility for my care during those early years. She would feed and bathe me and help with my daily care as a baby and toddler. When I was around three, she moved to Adelaide to live in supported accommodation. She fought for this opportunity, allowing her to learn vocational skills and enabling her to join the workforce and gain independent living skills. This helped her to adapt to life with a disability and to tap into resources that were never available in our country town.

It must have been a considerable adventure and experience for my sister to leave home and live so far away from her family at such a young age; there must have been times when she felt very alone, but the opportunities to meet new friends and learn new skills were invaluable to the rest of her life. Her options would have been limited if she had stayed in Broken Hill.

I remember highlights of my childhood with visits from my sister when she returned to Broken Hill on the *Greyhound* bus. We'd meet her at the bus station and seeing her was always the happiest moment – probably because I had grown so attached to her as a baby. She was the sophisticated big sister that I never thought of as disabled or blind like me; I think as our condition was a degenerative one, her eyesight was not significantly affected by daily activity. Therefore, it was never something we spoke about or even acknowledged. She would help me colour in and play games when she visited, and these times always seemed so special as someone was taking time to spend individual and quality time with me.

The departures were another story. I would always cry at our farewells. My parents would try to bribe me with an ice cream from the bus station café when she was leaving to stop me from being upset, but this did not work. I cried and still got the ice cream though.

My middle sister, a constant presence but distant due to the six-year age gap, played an enigmatic role in my life. She had little in common with her little sister. I remember times when we would play together in the yard or at the park, but as a general rule, she was always doing something different to me. I wonder how much she did for me that I never noticed or remembered.

She has a much more precise memory of our childhood than I do, and recently we had a conversation where she reminded me that I had imaginary friends as a child, even remembering what I named them. She said they were very present, and I would always wander around talking to them. This was because I was isolated as a child and probably made-up imaginary friends to keep myself occupied and for company.

My middle sister and I shared a bedroom together. We would have such big arguments about who was making the mess and who was in each other's space. There were great parts to this, too. I remember that once the lights were out, we often played word games before falling asleep. She tells me I used to sing to myself when she was trying to sleep, too, so I was an annoyance to her.

She had companionship from the girl who lived in the house across the vacant block from us. They were in the same year at school and would catch the bus together and hang out on many occasions outside school. The friendship my sister had with our neighbour made me jealous at times. It was unfair that my sister was allowed to have a friend, and I had to make up imaginary friends for myself.

Besides the neighbours, we were not permitted to have friends at our house after school or on weekends or holidays. My sister used to spend whatever time she could at the neighbour's house rather than ours. In my mind, it felt that my sister was always at the neighbour's house, but this is an exaggeration as I imagine that, in reality, my parents would have restricted her from going there too much.

My middle sister departed to live with my eldest sister and attend university in Adelaide after finishing high school. She left home when I was eleven and I loved the solitude and freedom of having no big sister spying on what I was doing and having a bedroom to myself. I made the best of it – using up all the room, taking over the space and making it my own. I felt so grown up and the sense of freedom in having my own space let me be more individual, spending my time and energy on things I enjoyed.

The trips to Adelaide for eye specialist appointments were always quite fun and a cherished little holiday until the anxiety of the actual appointment. Dad was often the one that would take me to Adelaide. Sometimes, we would drive for five hours, and sometimes, we'd catch the train or the *Greyhound* bus.

Once we were there, we would stay with my sisters and while they were at work or university, we would go on adventures. We often would visit the Adelaide Zoo and take a trip to Glenelg on the tram. We would walk along the beachfront and out onto the jetty.

These adventures around Adelaide with my dad are really fond memories. It was even more an opportunity to bond together than we had time for at home. I remember only a couple of other family holidays that were taken outside of visits to the eye specialist, so in some ways, these trips were the opportunity to travel that I would not have had if not for the disability.

The appointments, however, were like torture. In fact, sometimes, the machines that they put my head in to check on my eyes really did seem like a torture device. The eye drops were the worst thing as they used to sting. They always left me feeling more blind than I was, and the emotional side of this was the reminder that they really had no clue what was going on with my retina and that I would one day go totally blind.

It was not until I was much older, and my eldest sister attended a new specialist that she received the elusive diagnosis, which was followed up by me confirming this was the same for me. So now I can call it 'Rod Cone Dystrophy'. At least it has a name, and even though it is very nonspecific, having the diagnosis does make a difference.

Explaining what I can actually see and what I need help seeing is a tricky one. I have always had what is called night blindness. This means I cannot see in dark areas or dim lighting. One of the effects of this is that my eyes do not transfer from being in bright light to darkness quickly.

An easy way to imagine night blindness is by wearing dark sunglasses in an underground car park or a nightclub. This may be what it is like. It is difficult to explain something that I do not see as I have never seen what the alternative is that people without vision loss do see.

In essence, the brighter the environment I am in, the better I can see. I have never been able to see the stars in the sky, or what it may be like to play sport or drive a car.

When I was around seven, it was recommended by an eye specialist that I wear glasses. I found this a horrible experience. My family were never able to afford the more fashionable frames, so I always had the nasty plastic framed glasses which the kids at school would tease me about.

As the glasses were of little use to improve my eyesight, I would take them off when at school at every opportunity. I'm not sure how many conversations I had with my dad in relation to how my glasses got broken while they were in my schoolbag, but there were quite a few. The torment of the glasses lasted until I was in my first year of high school, when thankfully, another specialist advised that the glasses were really not helping and that they were no longer necessary.

What a relief.

Remembering to take the glasses off when I was dropped at school and keeping them safe in my bag all day and remembering to put them on again before I was collected at the end of the day was hard work. I am sure that Dad knew that I would not wear the glasses, but never directly had a conversation with me about this. For him, he thought the glasses were helpful and recommended so wanted me to wear them to help me, for me, the glasses were another way that I stood out and was different and gave the other kids another reason to be mean.

Over the years, my general vision has deteriorated as the light-sensing cells have died off. As my eyesight has gotten worse now, I can only see light and dark and sometimes detect bright colours if they are in my peripheral vision.

I have noticed that severe vision loss mostly happens at highly stressful times in my life. I am unsure if this is a psychophysical reaction to stress, but I now try my hardest to avoid stressful situations. What eyesight I have left is precious, and as I adapt, I learn different ways of managing daily tasks, but I definitely want to look after the remainder of the eyesight I have left as best I can.

Navigating childhood with a disability in Broken Hill demanded resourcefulness. It was important for us to utilise the few services available to access, which would have been more plentiful had we lived in a location not so remote. My parents took the attitude of letting me be the child who was not different due to my disability. Everyone adapted to make sure I was safe. I was looked after in the situations where my disability had an effect.

Generally, I was left to get on with life the best way I could and work out solutions to problems myself. This has made me very independent, resilient, and adaptable. It has also given me a self-belief that I can achieve what I want to do and push my boundaries to seek new adventures and reach my goals.

Dad would go to my school and make sure that the teachers I had each year gave me the support I required so I could be part of the classroom activities and learn like every other student. He would be there in the background, ensuring things ran smoothly.

Unfortunately, Dad was not able to counteract the discrimination and obstacles that came from those who were not able to accept my disability and create positive alternatives. He did, however, instil an attitude of resilience and emotional intelligence in me that gave me the skills to manage situations where many other children would have had relied upon adult support and intervention.

As my father was always around the home doing something, I tended to be his little shadow. He took up being a handyman in his spare time and would often help family and friends with household repairs and renovations. I would often tag along with these activities and learned how to lay concrete, tiles and carpet. I knew the basics of most household repairs and would usually be the one holding things or passing the required tools.

Dad was also an avid cook and would not only be in charge of the family dinners and making our school lunches, but also often bake goods such as cakes and pastries. It was not unusual to get up in the morning and find a batch of baked goods fresh out of the oven that I could have for breakfast or take to school for snacks. Not many kids ate scones fresh from the oven for breakfast or had homemade cupcakes to eat at morning break time. I was very fortunate.

As an early riser, Dad would often get half of the day's work done before we even woke up. I would sit with him and talk to him if he was cooking when I was awake. I never had the inclination to learn how to cook or bake myself, but I would love watching and helping out where I could.

I also used to love sitting with him at the kitchen table, watching him play Patience, as he used to call it, which we all know now as Solitaire. He would spend hours, especially during the winter months playing this. He would get me to tell him what moves to make next, and this game became a partnership rather than Solitaire. I guess this was one of his ways of getting me to think out different options and possibilities and develop critical thinking skills.

As my parents needed to be mindful of their finances, we never had any of the things that many other children had in our age group. Dad would do his best to make sure that we did not miss out entirely though, as he made us a home swing and slide set, would bring things home that he collected in his adventures and encourage us to use our imagination to create opportunities to play.

My parents were very much hands-off in the way that they supervised us. We were responsible for finding our own entertainment, which was generally outside activities, or if we were inside, it was not time spent watching television or movies. We never owned a home computer and as we were mostly solitary; we never interacted with other children much. I developed my love of books and music because these things can be done in solitude and did not cost much money.

I was never part of a sporting team, not only because of my disability but also because there was not that level of interaction with other children outside of the school scene. I was fascinated with basketball when I was eleven and pleaded for my parents to get me a ball and hoop.

Dad set me up a basketball ring nailed to the gum tree out the side of our house. It was unique. I could shoot hoops, bouncing my basketball on the red dirt and had a big old gum tree as a backboard. I joined the team at school for sports; the actual playing of basketball was not too tricky with my level of eyesight at the time, but then the competition against the other school team was held at the indoor basketball court and this was too dark for me to see in.

As a result, I was unable to play and had to sit on the sidelines. This built the belief in me that sports were not for me because I would never fit into what other people needed me to do to be part of a team.

My other love when I was this age was the trampoline. It was not the safety-minded trampolines they have now; it was the old-style rectangle mat with the springs exposed. We had it situated near the fence under the gum tree that was my basketball tree.

Left to my own devices and being the adventure seeker, I would jump off the fence onto the trampoline and do all sorts of tricks, getting the basketball and throwing it into the hoop from the trampoline. When my nephew or cousin would visit, I would make them fetch the basketball and throw it back to me to try again. I am sure I was the only blind eleven-year-old leaping off the fence with a basketball in my hands, doing a flip on the trampoline and sinking the basketball through the hoop. Totally dangerous but heaps of fun.

My disability did not impact me too much when I was young. At times, there were definitely things that I could not do. When it got dark and I was unable to see, my parents, middle sister, cousin, or nephew would have been responsible for making sure I did not fall over or hurt myself.

Having low vision at school was a difficult experience in that I could never read the blackboard. The other thing that excluded me were the purple printed stencils that many of us may remember from my age group. They smelled amazing when the teacher brought them in from the printer. Sometimes, they were okay to read, but in most circumstances, they were printed too faintly for me to see.

I would sit there sniffing the paper, but smell does not translate to sight. Those pages were only helpful to me if someone got a pen and wrote over the top of the print to make it darker. If someone did not do this, I would have to miss out on the activity, try to work out what was going on without the handout, or come up with something different to do. This only changed around Grade Five when the school started to use a photocopier to produce student handouts.

Sports day was always a complex arrangement for me in primary school; as a whole, I do not remember missing out on too much as my eyesight was at a level where I could participate in most activities. I think the teachers also had more scope in what they chose for us to do as a class – rather than having structured lesson plans for sports class. There were, however, times when the class would play sports such as cricket, which I could not participate in. I would be sent out to the outfield, even when my team was batting, and would be expected to fetch the ball if it happened to fly my way. Of course, this rarely occurred, so I would stand there in the hot sun for what seemed like an eternity simply being bored.

When it came to the whole school having sports time, I generally chose something like gymnastics or aerobics which was held at the school grounds, eliminating the need to participate in team activities and preventing additional costs to the family for participation in. I never learned to swim, so never attended the school swimming carnivals and as the athletics carnivals were generally held off site, I never attended these either.

Adapting to what was available to me and using my own imagination and creativity to fill in the gaps was the story of how I was able to navigate my way successfully through primary school. Many people assume that someone that is blind, or who would go blind, would learn how to read Braille. For me, this was not an option as there was no one that lived in Broken Hill that was skilled to teach me Braille. It is like learning any foreign language, in that it is best to learn when you are young.

When I was in Grade Three, at around eight years of age, I was introduced to typing. I am unsure now who suggested that I learn to type. I started on one of the very old-style typewriters where you needed to press the mechanical keys.

By the time I reached Grade Four, the education department had sponsored a modern typewriter with a soft press keyboard. I found the typing lessons so boring and detested the touch-type learning activities. I was always looking at the keys on the typewriter and trying to finish the exercise as fast as possible.

A specialist teacher would come in once a week for an hour and take me to a spare classroom for typing lessons. She got so frustrated with me looking at the keys that she purchased a roll of blue sticky dots and stuck one on every letter key of the keyboard. I had no option but to learn to type then. That teacher must have been so patient to put up with me telling her how boring typing lessons were and how I was never going to need to use the typing skills.

By the time I reached Grade Six, I could not participate in music class as it required reading from the blackboard or a music chart from the wall that I could not see. The alternative was to attend the school library in these times and practice my typing – where I finally upgraded to using a computer. I would do my mandatory typing lesson and then use the rest of the time to write short stories. I would print them out and hand them to the librarian to read.

Sometimes I wrote so much that the dot matrix printer with the roll of paper would run out of pages because I wrote such long 'short' stories. How patient that librarian was to read all of my work.

The highlight of Grade Six was becoming more popular with my classmates. Before this, I only had one or two friends, and they often ended up in a lower academically graded class than me. This was also probably a reflection of the socio-economic background of these students. Even though I was always in classes with people that I matched with academically, I did not have the things that made me fit in such as the latest toys, stationary or gadgets.

I always felt left out.

I feel that the kids from the lower classes did not worry so much about the differences we had as none of us had the things that made us 'cool', and my disability was just another part of the things that made me not cool – rather than seen as a separate problem.

In Grade Six, I was accepted by people in my own class for the first time ever. We had an athletics carnival held at the school rather than the athletics ground, and I was permitted to attend. Surprisingly, I came first or second in some of the track and field events.

Before this, no one had ever thought of me as a sportsperson, which is no surprise, as even I had never thought of myself as a person that could be good at sports. I was asked to represent my school at the inter-school competition. I was successful at this event too, however, was not permitted by my parents to attend the regional competition.

The other highlight was our annual *Jump Rope for Heart* day. I could do all the tricks with the double skipping ropes and remember it was a great day. I even contributed to the music played over the school sound system as a family friend had copied me some tapes with the most recent chart music on them. The highlight of this was not the event itself but the inclusion and my participation with others.

I fondly look back on Grade Six as the best year of my schooling because I was accepted by my classmates. I still had my other friends to hang out with during break, but I was also included and could feel like part of the class group. I was also approached to be a library monitor and prided myself in being part of something that felt important.

Amazingly, I managed to retrieve the Grade Six school and library monitor photos from the house fire salvage. They are scarred with smoke damage, but they are good memories. I left primary school with a sense of great things to come. The kids were seemingly more accepting and I thought, somewhat foolishly, that high school would be even better.

Our primary school graduation had been a fun event with all of us feeling like we were moving onto something bigger and better. I had been permitted to spend the day at my friend's house for the first time ever, which was really exciting and made me feel like I was doing the same things as everyone else my age. I was even invited to a classmate's birthday party during the summer holidays, especially exciting as it was one of the popular girls.

I had been given some new hand-me-down clothes that were fitting of the current fashion, and I had my music, books, friends at school and my own space at home to personalise. I would read *Dolly* and dream of all the things ahead of me that life had to bring.

Besties and Bullies

Primary school had left me with a false sense of security. I had no idea what lay ahead of me at high school; no idea of the harsh lessons that life was going to bring my way. I always knew that my disability and my life circumstances made me different to others my own age, but falsely thought that I could fit in. I was sure that I could be like my favourite book characters and would have the usual concerns of being a teen, friends, relationships, love, parties, and fashion.

Oh, if only this could have been the case.

Getting up every morning in high school and mustering the energy to put my best face forward was not always easy. Trying to fit in and be part of the crowd was time-consuming and exhausting. There were numerous reasons why fitting in was impossible; looking back, this was like trying to reach an unattainable goal. Instead, I ended up with moments where I was isolated and withdrawn, these times overshadowing the good times and leaving bitter memories.

My experiences of mean-spirited behaviours in primary school were nothing in comparison to the harsh reality of high school. One hears the horror stories and sees the scenes unfold in movies where the cruel kids wreak havoc, yet there is a comforting resolution where the tables turn, leading to a happy ending. Little did I know that my story would follow a different script.

The cruelty I encountered surpassed my expectations and the impact of others' actions and words ran so deep that it convinced me of my own worthlessness, leaving me with a sense of having no value and casting a shadow of gloom over my high school experience.

Broken Hill filters the primary schools into two high schools based on location. Although our house was on the south side of the piles of dirt in the middle of town, our designation was the high school in the north. My middle sister, who was now at university, had attended this school, and it was my turn. She had warned me that high school might be difficult, but after the rosy ending to my primary schooling, I felt invincible and sure that high school would be a different experience for me.

Classes were graded, leaving me without any of my childhood friends from primary school. The others from my class in Grade Six who had shown some element of friendship the previous year either were outside my class grouping or seemed to realise that I was unpopular again and it was not in their best interest to show me support.

Walking in on the first day with so many unfamiliar faces around me, I felt isolated and worried but still hopeful. I sat at the front of the class, desperately hoping I would be lucky enough to have someone else to sit with and make a new friend. No such luck. Our homeroom class was the same designation as the rest of our classes and there were no friendly faces anywhere.

This was not getting off to a good start.

I still held a glimmer of hope that something would change, and someone would offer friendship but as the days passed, this seemed less and less likely and my hopes and dreams of high school friendships faded.

My primary school friends and I organised a catch-up location and we would meet at break times, sharing stories of what was happening in our lives. There was an ever-increasing number of tales that involved people I did not know. We still had plenty in common that involved old stories or jokes and we were able to maintain our friendships to some extent. However, it was obvious that the commonalities were becoming less by the day.

As everyone settled into high school and the kids who needed to assert their authority started to emerge, it was plain to everyone that I was isolated from others and became an easy target. My socio-economic background again impacted as all the other students in my class were able to fit in with the latest trends, or where they did not, they had support and friendship from others in the class to protect them from the bullies.

My disability also made me different from the other kids. The taunts became a common occurrence. Sometimes, mean comments were directed at me when we were lined up outside a classroom to go in. Other times, it was a conversation that would take place with several students in the school room once we were all seated.

They would either ask me questions that embarrassed me for the whole class to hear or would name-call, point and gossip about me loudly amongst themselves. This would occur if the teacher were present or not. The teachers simply could not protect me or discipline the troublemakers. This lack of support from teachers and the system exacerbated the pain, leaving me feeling powerless and unworthy.

I recall a few incidents that stand out from the rest. One of these was a bad hair day from hell that, on anyone else, may have been funny, but for me, it was a disaster. My fringe needed a cut, and as Dad had done this many times before, I asked him to trim my fringe. Little did I know that he maybe had a glass of wine or three and cut it too short. Perhaps he had just had enough of me whinging about my hair in my face and thought he would be super helpful. Whatever it was, the result was the same, and as hard as you may wish, hair cannot be stuck back on once it is chopped off.

This was when spiky, gelled fringes were a thing, but I did not have any gel, and as it had not been done by a hairdresser, the spiky something did not work. So, I was stuck with super short fringe; to make matters worse, it was the day before school photo day. So, there is a permanent reminder of the bad haircut. I was embarrassed. The other kids thought it hilarious and, of course, another thing to add to the list of things to tease me about. Thank goodness hair grows back, so this was a temporary point to tease me on. There were plenty of other things the kids would do that were frustrating and all seemed to add to my misery.

Moving my schoolbag from where I had put it at break time so I could not find it again was a favourite. Another was turning off the classroom lights as I was walking to my desk in the class. As the school had limited or no windows in the inner classrooms, I suddenly could not see my way to the desk and would bump into things on the way.

Kids would put their feet out, so I would trip as I went by them in the corridor or step in front of me at the last moment and then abuse me for walking into them. The other favourite tick was to flick my pen off the desk as they walked past and then watch me scrabble around on the floor, trying to find it by feel. These things were small and petty, but they would add up.

The worst were mean words and the constant reminder that I was different and would never fit in. This exclusion was not only a social thing but was often made worse by the inability of the mainstream education system to understand the needs of someone with a disability.

In particular, one boy seemed to prioritise making my life miserable. He was generally the ringleader when it came to the group teasing and taunting that would happen either in the classroom or in the corridor as I walked past. I hate to say it, but later on, this boy had a motorbike accident when we were in Grade Nine and never returned to school afterwards. I was not pleased that he had hurt himself, but there was a little bit of me silently thanking the universe for taking him away from being able to torment me.

I found one refuge, which was the haven of the school library. I was in awe at all the books and opportunities this gave me for a temporary escape. When my friends were busy doing something else, or I needed time to myself as I had been punished by the bullies where I craved solitude, I would go find a book and quiet spot in the corner of the library and hang out with my friends the books.

The librarian always looked out for me. Having someone supporting me and giving me a safe refuge to hide in made the difference. She often overlooked me being in the library when students were not supposed to be there.

Grade Seven was the worst year of my schooling and was not improved by the house burning down halfway through the school year. With hand-me-down clothes, this gave the mean kids another thing that made me stand out from the crowd and a topic for the relentless teasing.

There was an opportunity for me to change high schools when we moved to our new house, as it was zoned for the other high school. I pondered the prospect of a fresh start but decided it was better to work with what I already knew. Broken Hill, being the size it was, there was no guarantee that there would not be friends of the mean kids at the other school that would continue the torment. The school was also all in one building, which made navigation easy.

In contrast, the other high school had many separate buildings, so I convinced the principal to let me stay as I had started the year and now was familiar with the teachers and the school layout. This meant that Dad needed to drive me to school and pick me up each day as the school was too far to walk and the school buses did not go near my new house.

The meanest girl in the class was the most difficult to manage as she would exploit the vulnerabilities girls worried about and then use them to tease me. Pimples, my clothes, even though we had a school uniform, and the fact I could not write notes in class from the blackboard. You name it, and she would find that point of weakness to target. Imagine how devastated I was to find out she lived across the road when we moved to our new house.

I am not sure why she was out of the school zone, but this now meant that I was not safe even at home. I was often sent to the local service station to collect milk or the newspaper, and I was always terrified to think that I would encounter her along the way. I convinced myself she was waiting around the corner, ready to leap out to attack me every time.

The following year was a breath of fresh air. We were assigned to classes where they were mixed, not according to grades. This meant I had one girl from my group of friends in my homeroom and a central set of classes. It is incredible that having that one friend made things so much easier. It does not mean that the bully kids stopped their torment, but it did mean that I at least had a friend to distract me and make me feel less alone.

After a week or so in our new English class, I met Peter. He was sitting with another boy I knew from primary school in the seats in front of us, and we were put in a group exercise together. I knew in an instant that Peter was a lovely person. He was such a kind and understanding soul who made you feel comfortable as though you had known him forever.

English class became quite pleasant from then on as I loved English as a subject, and now, I had friends. This did not mean that it was always good, and there were still moments when the mean kids took control of my comfort, but as a whole, it was significantly better. Maybe it was that I had resigned to school being a terrible experience and had built an expectation that when the moments came along that it was manageable, it would seem much better than it was.

Getting bullied left me with a constant feeling of being inferior and insecure; it makes you constantly on guard and trying to protect yourself, even when there is no current threat; it is the perceived threat or the need to ensure that you give the mean kids nothing to work with.

Halfway through the year, we had a re-grading for our math and science classes. I was graded up in science and taken to a new class. I sat in the only spare seat in the class at a table with five other girls I had never met before. The girl that sat next to me introduced herself as Dee and she seemed really lovely.

Soon, Dee and I became friends in class and would speak about our schoolwork and pair up for practical experiments. My disability seemed to not phase her, and she was happy to take control of the practical activities – such as using the Bunsen burner – and I would write the notes.

The teachers had banned me from using the Bunsen burners as they seemed to think I would burn down the school, so I was lucky to have a partner willing to work with me. And we made a pretty good team. We would go our separate ways when the class finished, but this was another class in which I now had a companion.

At the time of the grading, our math class had a new girl introduced. As the only spare seat in the class was next to me, she came and took the place, introducing herself as Kirsty. Instantly, we became friends.

We would not only share information about the math class but also started to share personal insights. I love how sometimes you just meet someone, and that connection occurs instantly. This was what it was like for me with Kirsty. She did not care too much what others thought and seemed on her own journey.

She was a musician and artist, and this creativity helped her not to worry so much about fitting in. It gave her more ability to just do her own thing. She invited me to join her and her friends at lunch break. As the tendrils of friendship had been weakening with the girls I had been friends with in primary school, this was a great invitation.

I told my old friends I had been invited to hang out with some new people and would still spend some time with them, but I wanted to spend time with a new group. Much to my delight and surprise, when Kirsty introduced me to her best friend, it was none other than Dee from my science class. We laughed and decided that this must have been fate.

Soon after Peter joined our group, I realised he was also a musician, and all of my new friends already knew each other and were happy to have me slot into their group. This was so exciting and scary at the same time. I had never been invited to be part of a friend's group before, which meant so much. I always checked in on my old friends, but gradually, they all left school for various reasons, so the choice to take the risk with new friends certainly was the right one for me.

As all of the group I was now spending time with were musicians, I decided that I would like to join the music class and the choir. We had no family funds to purchase an instrument, but I could use the piano at school. The donations from the house fire contained a small electronic keyboard that I could use at home to practice on.

My mother would frown at using the keyboard, so I would take the opportunity to practice after school when I did not have other chores to do. Dad supported the music and would use some of the grocery money to purchase the lesson books when I needed them. I eventually had to give up music class as the teacher expected I would sight-read music. The curriculum defined that I would need to sight-read a piece of music for my exams.

As I was not able to do this with my disability, the teacher did not consider any reasonable adjustment he could make to help. I found out later that there were things such as large print or braille music sheets. I had no choice but to remove myself from the class; otherwise, I would have failed.

The day I got the teacher to sign me off from the course, I took the one and only time to stand up for myself and advocate. The conversation went something like, *"I could have been the next Stevie Wonder, for all you know."*

He just looked at me in amazement as I walked away. Had he never considered that music is universal and that people who have a disability are just as capable as others? Probably not. Hopefully, I gave him some food for thought. This, however, meant that I needed to join another class I had no friends in again. Advanced math was a subject that had ten boys and one girl, so I ended up having a person to talk with in class, as the girls stuck together to some extent.

Another friend who joined our group was JR. I knew him from primary school, and we had a lot in common in that he was also teased incessantly at school due to his perceived sexual orientation. It is strange how kids will find something to tease about even when they have no idea what it means. Before hormones, JR used to have a tough time. We had some extra level of understanding for each other and our circumstances. We now had the opportunity to build a friendship never quite reached in primary school.

The first time I was allowed to go out with my friends, Kirsty, Dee, JR, Peter, and I went to the movies. It was a double feature, and we were so excited. Movies took ages to screen at the movie theatre; it would have been better to wait for the video release most of the time. But going to the movies with my friends made me feel so grown up. Another of those rites of passage that seem inconsequential to most, but for me a chance to prove myself to be like everyone else and fit in.

My parents trusted that my friends would look after me, and we had a parent who would pick us up afterwards and drive us home. Saturday night out with my friends made me feel sophisticated and included in a group. For everyone else, they had been doing this since they were kids.

It was my first time, and I was determined to make it the best night ever.

We got our snacks and found seats. My friends ensured that I was okay with our seating location and guided me safely through the dark movie theatre. At the end of the movie, we were all so happy. It had been a fantastic night.

My friends led me in the dark towards our designated pick-up location, which meant crossing the road. As teenagers, we chose not to walk to the traffic lights, but decided to cross the road mid-block. As we began the crossing, a car came up the road, and so, of course, my friends told me to run. They did not tell me, though, that there was a median strip in the middle of the road, which I managed to fall over. My friends all kept running.

Everyone was so embarrassed when they realised I had fallen over. Looking back, they probably felt a little guilty but mostly embarrassed. Me, I was mortified. What was a great night out now had me falling face first on the road in the main street. Everyone would know about this – another thing I would be teased about when I went to school on Monday.

Peter came back to help me up, and we tried to laugh it off, but for me, it was the dampener on a great night. I had been out with my friends, but in the same instance, I had proved that my disability would always have an impact.

How would I cope the rest of my life if I could not attend the movies without a disaster?

Suddenly, this event had gone from a fun night out where I was proving my independence to a night when that independence and all other things for my future became questionable.

Like many families in Broken Hill, Dee and her family lived there because of her father's job. Once his contract expired, the family decided to return to live in Sydney, where they had lived previously. This was a loss as it is a huge deal when you only have a few friends, and one leaves. We stayed in contact via writing letters for a while, but as Dee made new friends and reconnected with people from her past, we lost touch.

The rest of junior high school went along the same path as Grade Eight. I had some classes with friends and some courses without. I decided to be as best academically as possible and follow my dreams and goals. I was not strong in the creativity and arts area, so when my friends chose classes focused on art, I selected the humanities subjects as electives. Even though this meant I was by myself away from my support network, I had grown used to the bullies. I had developed coping mechanisms to just keep focused on the schoolwork and to ignore the taunts and bullying as much as possible. And when it got too much, I would return to my refuge in the library.

My friends and I would spend hours talking to each other outside of school. Except for special occasions, I could not visit them for after-school catchups, so we made the best of the phone. There were no such things as conference calls, so we would all arrange to talk to each other at a specific time, speak to one friend, and then call the other friend to confirm information or make arrangements for some activity at school the following day.

Peter would always be told to get off the phone by his stepfather as he would try to call home to check in and always get a busy signal. He could never understand why, after spending all day at school together, we needed to talk again after school. Those phone calls were the times when I got to spend individual moments with my friends and to be able to build the support and have that feedback that friends give to look after each other. Most kids would just hang out at each other's houses, but as I was not permitted to do this, phone conversations were my lifeline.

The highlight of Grade Ten was the high school prom. I was desperate to go as the rest of the year attended. Prom was, to me, one of those benchmark moments in life. All the characters in books and movies went to prom – even the unpopular kids. It is a rite of passage.

Peter and Kirsty were going together. My friends all chipped in to buy me a ticket to attend. My mother forbade me from attending, stating we could not get a dress, and I am not sure to this day what her other reasons were. Unlike Cinderella, no fairy godmother came to take me to the ball. In essence, this was another potential disaster adverted. If I had of attended it could have been a remake of the movie *Carrie* – though, maybe not as dramatic, but with some horrible consequences nonetheless – so hindsight tells me that non-attendance at the Grade Ten prom was a good outcome.

I shut myself in my bedroom and spent the night wondering about all the fun stuff happening without me. I was so sad and angry that I was not allowed to attend. There were still enough people who wanted to make my life difficult in attendance. There was no way I would have been able to have a new dress or meet the expectations to fit into a formal without more resources than I had. I was better off staying home than being the point of everyone's taunts It was however, one of those times when the divide between myself and the others became obvious. Even though I knew that I did not fit in, I was so desperate to do so, I simply wanted to be like everyone else and was so sad and frustrated that the Prom was another one of those things that due to my circumstances I would never have as a memory.

As time passed, fewer and fewer kids who did not want to be at school were in attendance. Either they were old enough to quit, got a job, or had other reasons for leaving. By the end of Grade Ten and junior high school, many people making my life difficult took the opportunity to leave rather than attend the senior high school studies.

This was a relief; it meant everyone remaining was indifferent to me and just got on with their own thing. There were a few new students, and these people were old enough to not worry so much about gossip and rumours and doing mean things.

At this time, I also grew more aware of how to better manage my disability and communicate my needs to the teaching staff. Sports classes were removed and my disability impacted less on the day-to-day classroom activities.

In Grade Eleven, an exchange student from Finland came and spent a few months with us. At the end of her exchange, a big farewell party was organised at the local community hall. The invitation was open to everyone who had been part of her community while she was with us.

JR and I decided to attend. Again, we were trying to fit in and be like everyone else. The party was fun but very daunting. All the kids indifferent to me over the years were the same, still unconcerned. They were surprised to see me at an event out of school, but that was the only blip on the radar. No one was mean or questioned why I was there, which was a relief.

I was really uncomfortable and the biggest wallflower that night, but I was also happy to have attended. There were a few people who were friendly enough to acknowledge us. Even though I spent much of the night hanging out away from the loud music and dark dancefloor area only lit by party lights, there were moments when I was included and people actually came and started conversations with me, to my utter amazement. There was a cake and some speeches; everyone felt nostalgic and sad.

At the time, there was a song called *'Forever'* in the charts by Mariah Carey. We all got in a big circle with arms linked over the following person's shoulder. We had a group sing the song, swaying along to the music in a big circle. It was all very teary and sad and has stayed memorable; I am unsure if it was because this was a shared moment of emotion or if it impacted me so much for other reasons.

After all, the exchange student was leaving, but this was the first time I had been included in any large group and accepted. That night was all about the exchange student but also about me. It showed me that there were times when I could be accepted, and as long as I kept to the sidelines and did not make myself stand out, as long as there was a distraction, and as long as I behaved like everyone else, I could be part of the crowd.

To extend our studies for the specialist classes, we had attendance at school in the evening hours. Twice a week, I had a subject that required me to be at school from 6pm until 7pm. First, I would walk to school and then get a taxi home. Later, I had friends who were beginning to get their licences, and I was able to get a lift, which again made me feel included and like everyone else.

It is funny looking back now. I was never allowed to have a push bike, but my mother agreed to me getting a lift to and from school with Peter or JR. You would think that teenagers in cars have the possibility of going much more wrong from a safety perspective than me riding a push bike.

On the night that neither JR nor Peter was there, another student realised I was catching a taxi and offered to give me a ride home as he would drive past my house. I was so happy and realised that by this time, people were less worried about what others thought and were beginning to treat people as people, regardless of their circumstances.

By the final year of school, we had reduced our numbers to the kids who wanted to be there. Those who wanted to go on to follow a life, university or a career where the final year of school was required. A larger group of people who were comfortable in themselves, kids who were not popular, not sporty, not super academic but who had a purpose. Those who had all generally experienced some of the harsh results of being a teenager either through what life had dealt them outside of school, or from the bullies that had made their lives hell across the junior years, all started to bond together.

We had a designated area where, even if you were not with your best friends, you could go to the area and still find someone to sit with. Sometimes, you would chat; other times, you would simply be together in the space doing your own thing, reading a book, doing some schoolwork, or just sitting while others had a conversation. It was a place that felt safe and somewhere that there was no judgment.

For me, the friends were the saviour that took the school from being a torture place – that I was at times scared and so sad to attend, even though I loved learning – into a place that was manageable with the people around me. I managed to keep my focus on what was important which I knew was my schoolwork and getting the marks to reach my goal of leaving Broken Hill for university.

Today, we have a school system that manages bullies – although I'm sure that mean kids still exist. The behaviours may be even more covert or occur on social media now. As teens, personal identity and being included as part of the pack is so important. It is a balance that is sometimes reached without much difficulty. For others, such as myself, it was a constant battle of trying to balance my emotions – while trying to fit social norms and have the same experiences as I saw others undertaking.

It's sad that I cannot reflect upon much of my high school as happy; I have consciously chosen to forget much of the day-to-day things as it was so unpleasant. The shining light in all of the difficult times are the moments shared with friends. These friendships have lasted the years and Kirsty, Peter and I still catch up on a regular basis when we are in the same city.

If it had not been for the branches of friendship that were extended, I am sure that my experience of high school may have been unbearable and caused me to leave without ever reaching my goals.

The Blind Leading the Blind

"*What? Go to Sydney all by myself on a plane?*"

The question I asked when it was suggested that my support from *Vision Australia* was better provided by a visit for a week for me at the twice-yearly recreational camps.

Since I had been in primary school, a social worker from *Vision Australia* had made the trip to Broken Hill twice a year. It was a waste of resources when this involved days out of the office, flights, accommodation, car hire and a willingness to want to travel to the other side of the state. The idea to bring me to the camp was a no-brainer from a resource perspective.

What an adventure for me!

At fourteen, it would be my first time leaving my family. This excursion promised a welcome break for me and a respite for my parents from the incessant nagging that often occurred when I was on school holidays. I was always bored and looking for something to keep me busy around the house.

The prospect of an all-expenses paid holiday was too good to pass up – even if it required serious persuasion from the social worker. Convincing my parents on such matters took a lot of work, and I can only imagine the skilled negotiations to secure this opportunity.

In the weeks leading up to the departure date, I was consumed with anticipation for the journey ahead. Excitement bubbled inside me whenever I thought about the adventure I was about to embark upon. I packed and repacked my suitcase over several weeks, trying to decide what I needed to take with me. I was so enthusiastic that I couldn't resist sharing my boundless excitement with my friends at school. I am sure I became a constant presence in their ears, painting vivid pictures of my upcoming solo flight and the wonders that awaited me during the holidays.

The day I set off for my first camp, Dad drove me to the little airport in Broken Hill. Standing there, bidding him farewell, I couldn't shake the sensation of newfound maturity. With a sense of grown-up responsibility, he wished me a good trip and left me with an airline attendant to walk me toward the awaiting plane.

The attendant directed me to my seat on the plane, and to my relief, it was not one of those cramped spaces, and the plane was bigger than I had expected. As I settled in, I braced myself for what promised to be the most significant adventure of my young life. Glancing around at my fellow passengers, it struck me that I was the only person of my age group in a cabin predominately occupied by business professionals.

Before the widespread accessibility of air travel to the general population – particularly on regional air services – taking to the skies was a luxury reserved for those who travelled for work or were wealthy. The fact that I was travelling by myself added an extra layer to the uniqueness of this experience.

After a take-off I found exhilarating, I recall gazing out of the aircraft window, marvelling at the landscape below. Watching us fly over the local farmland and the vast expanse of red earth as the plane ascended into the clouds. As the landscape disappeared from view, I turned my attention to a book, feigning an air of sophistication while secretly bubbling with excitement.

Time seemed to slip away, and soon, we were circling and coming into land. The thrill of spotting the ocean through the plane window overcame me; everything below seemed immense and grand, leaving me excited. Every moment of that descent held a particular moment in my memory.

What fascinated me most was the sheer number of people rushing about. Never before had I been surrounded by such a bustling crowd, dwarfing the experiences of my visits to Adelaide. The impact of this lively atmosphere left a lasting impression on me.

Upon arrival, my social worker greeted me at the airport and whisked me to her house for an overnight stay. The camp was scheduled to start on Sunday morning, but my Friday afternoon flight availability necessitated my early arrival.

As we indulged in a pizza dinner, my social worker and her husband kindly offered suggestions. They asked about my preferences for our activities the following day.

There were endless possibilities.

We decided on a trip to the city, the tourist icon tour was in order. Our plan was simple but so wonderful. A stroll around the city, taking in the landmarks such as the Harbour Bridge and Opera House, possibly a movie, following no specific plan, just going where our feet took us.

That night, I slept in the spare room but did not get much sleep. I had a *Walkman* with me and realised that radio in Sydney had numerous stations, and they all played recent chart music – especially on a Friday night. I remember laying there scrolling from station to station, listening to my favourite music from the charts and thinking that something so simple was so unique.

Broken Hill had one radio station at the time and rarely played the music from the chart. Every time I thought I would go to sleep *'after this song'*, another song would play that I loved and another and another.

Preparing to kick off the day, I found myself void of that peculiar, weird sense of protocol when staying at someone else's house. The moment I sensed my hosts awake, I bounced out of bed, instantly geared up to embrace the new day, regardless of my lack of sleep.

We decided to watch the newly released *Madonna* movie. JR was a huge fan of Madonna. I kept my movie butts for him; something else I had never seen was movie butts with the name of the movie and cinema on it.

After the movie, we wandered around the city, looking at all the attractions. I loved the hustle and bustle and was so excited to have this experience that made me feel like I had the world at my fingertips. The social worker and her husband were captured by my enthusiasm and kept taking me to show me different things around the city. We went to places that showed me things I had never even dreamed existed, and the simple things like the tall buildings were terrific to me.

You can always tell a kid from the country when they go to the city as they look up at the buildings in awe – no one that has grown up in the city ever does this. I was so interested in all the different people from different cultures and, in many cases, seeing people from international destinations I had never experienced before. I instantly fell in love with the city and, on that day, decided that Sydney was a place that I would visit more often, or maybe even live in one day.

After another night of scrolling through radio stations – which also included some more sleep – it was time to prepare to meet the other people I would spend the upcoming week with at camp.

We all gathered together in the car park at *Vision Australia* and my social worker introduced me to a few people before we boarded the minibuses. Everyone was friendly with each other, and many of them were already acquainted. Preferring to keep to myself, I allowed my inherent shyness to take the lead.

Taking a seat on the bus, I was relieved to escape the awkward social intricacies of not knowing anyone. The social worker had assured me that there were other newcomers to the camp, easing my apprehension. Still, fear lingered that, much like my frosty initiation into high school, the promise of something good could unravel.

I must admit I was also quite overwhelmed by the fact that this was the first time I had ever seen blind people. Other than at night, my daily eyesight was still not too bad; therefore, I was probably one of the kids with a better range of vision. Some relied on others for sighted guide assistance, while others used long, white canes.

I had never seen this before and certainly had never understood that there were other kids my own age who were blind. My social worker had this underlying concept when inviting me to attend. Not only did it mean that she did not have to come to Broken Hill, but I would also have an opportunity to meet others in a similar situation and learn something from the experience.

As teenagers, we are in a constant state of comparison and self-judgement against others. The thing was that living where I did, which was so remote, I had never encountered other people that were my own age who had a similar disability. I had spent all my time comparing myself to others who were not in my situation. People at school, people in magazines or on the television. Not people who were also teenagers who were blind.

All of a sudden, I had other kids that were like me. We all had different diagnoses, but the underlying issue affecting us all was the same.

We journeyed up to the Central Coast, about one and a half hours north of Sydney. Peering out of the bus window, I was captivated by the surroundings. There was so much to see and take in. The city as we drove through it, the traffic, the buildings, and the infrastructure like bridges over rivers. And then we entered an area of trees. Trees so tall that I could not see the top of them from the bus window. Trees everywhere, like a forest. This dense treescape was nothing like I had ever witnessed.

In Broken Hill, scattered gum trees or those strategically planted by the city council for shade were the extent of my tree encounters. The abundance and majesty of these trees on this journey was a spectacle. The day before, I was the girl from the country looking up at the tall buildings; now, I was the girl trying to see the tops of the trees; everything seemed tall and on a different scale from what I was used to.

On arrival at the location we were to call home for the coming week, I was even more excited. The area was laid out with shared dormitory cabins in the bushland. There were clear walking paths, and it all seemed easy to navigate. In the excitement, though, there was still some trepidation about what we would be doing and, of course, the people I would be sharing time with.

What if this was just like school and the people did not like me? What if I did not fit in and did not make any friends?

Suddenly, I missed the predictability of Broken Hill so far away. Realising I had taken on something that I could not change now, I had to embrace the situation rather than worry about the outcome as it was not something I could change.

We all congregated in the large hall, where the social workers made some basic introductions and the generic get-to-know-you activities. About thirty of us ranged across different years of high school up to Grade Eleven. The kids doing Grade Twelve were not invited due to study requirements.

As we did our introduction and icebreaker activities, I tried to remember everyone's name – especially those the same age as me. There was a group of three girls sitting together that seemed nice; however, you could tell they were the popular girls, and I knew I had no chance of being part of their group. I hoped they did not take a dislike to me and would not turn out to be mean.

To my surprise, when the dorm allocations were read out, I had been allocated a room with these girls. We collected our bags from where they had been offloaded from the buses and went to claim our beds. When I walked into the room, I was presented with one of the popular girls literally bounding up to me and saying, *"Hi, I am Renee. Do you like having fun?"*

I was astounded.

"Of course, I like fun," I replied nervously.

"Great. Well, you are now our friend!"

How easy was that? I thought to myself.

This girl seemed cool, popular, and pretty and invited me to be her friend. Wow. It was like I had walked into some kind of twilight zone. Renee introduced her other friends to me, Karen, and Tess, and from that moment onward, we were inseparable for the rest of our camp years together.

During camp, I found myself embraced as one of the popular kids. Others of varying ages, both older and younger, gravitated to me, eager for my friendship, attention, and acceptance. Along with Renee, we were considered role models, and the ones others would seek out for companionship.

What a contrast to what I had experienced at school. It was a moment to reflect and suddenly understand that all the things I had been striving so hard for socially just happened at camp and that if people accepted me, maybe I was actually likeable.

What a strange thought that suddenly, I could influence my social interactions and others.

I became the person people would come to for advice; besides my friends at school, this was my first time in this position. It was a little overwhelming, but at the same time, I felt so proud that I could just be myself and that others liked me for who I was. The camp was an opportunity for a clean slate, as no one knew my situation back in Broken Hill and could not judge me. I could choose what to tell people and what to keep to myself about my life at home and school and be able to let them take me at face value.

It was a chance for us all to experiment with being 'normal' teenagers in a safe environment. Many of the people at camp struggled socially interacting with others, and this group was where we all helped and supported each other.

Spending time with the other people at camp gave me the understanding that I could be anything I wanted to be and to take on anything that any other person my age could do – possibly even more. We participated in many activities that week that I had never had the opportunity to do. Horse riding, boat driving on the river, abseiling, and even four-wheel bike riding.

These are not only activities that many would question if a blind person should be participating in from a safety perspective but also activities that others our age would never have had the opportunity to do. The social workers and the activity providers guided the activities, but we all worked together. For those like me who had more eyesight, we would help the others who needed more assistance as their vision was more limited or they were totally blind.

For me, it would then flip at night-time when my night blindness kicked in, and we would all help each other as much as possible. You would think this seemed dangerous, with literally the blind leading the blind, but we made it work, and it made us all develop better relationships and ways to work together.

This is not to say that everyone was always friends; there were sometimes minor conflicts, but never anything serious or caused long-term arguments. No one was ever teased for their disability, and on the whole, we were all very kind and considerate of each other's feelings.

Of course, when you throw teenage hormones in the mix, there were plenty of people who wanted to be more than friends. It was no different from other teenagers who spent time together at a camp. It was like the books and the movies I had seen of the kids who attended holiday camps. Scary and daunting at the beginning, but the rewards and social interactions, not to mention lifelong friendships, were so worth that anxiety. I was just like the lead character in the story or movie, who had experienced something that was even better than fiction and changed my life.

Evening activities often included sessions where we would discuss topics in small groups. These were the items that we were potentially facing difficulty with due to our disability, home, or school situation. We had one evening expressly delegated as the 'Deep and Meaningful Night'.

We all used to roll our eyes and think these sessions were too serious and thought-provoking, but we knew they were also beneficial. I was amazed that the other kids also had bullies at school. Even my popular friend Renee was treated differently at her school. These sessions allowed us all to share ideas and talk through what was happening to us.

It was a time to realise that you were not alone and that sometimes someone else solved a problem you had never thought of. One of the key ideas I got from these sessions was to write a note to provide to the class teacher at the beginning of the year. This meant that at the beginning of each new class in the first week, I could hand the message to the teacher explaining my disability and the required assistance.

This meant it was subtle, and the rest of the class did not have to hear the conversation. It also meant that I did not have an uncomfortable conversation, which made me vulnerable. Such a small thing, but it made the difference in what had been a challenging interaction into something that was communicated clearly without any angst on my part.

We also had the opportunity to ponder our future and think about what we wanted to do. Until then, I had thought I wanted to be a journalist. It was exciting to hear the dreams of my fellow campers and to understand that some of them had been supported in following their dreams and others, such as me, had little support or expectation of the future. I never imagined how many options there were out there. I also had no idea that so many resources and things could help us on the journey. Resources available in the city that I had yet to learn even existed.

As my vision deteriorated over the years while I attended camps, we were able to share ideas on how I could use adaptive technology or what options we had for adjustments, like extra time for exams for high school.

The positive environment was also an incredible boost to understanding personal capacity. At the time, I was one of the kids with more vision than many others. But my mental state was far from positive. I had been taught that people with disabilities do not get real jobs, have a career, or live life doing the things that everyone else does. Part of me had not given this much thought before going to the camps.

I was probably living in some alternative fictional reality where part of me thought I could do everything without ever considering how practical it was.

I lived so much of my life escaping from reality into books because my reality was not a nice place to be, so a realistic view of the future had never been considered. Some kids at the camp were totally blind and were managing their daily lives and plans for the future much better than I was. I was influenced by the idea that there is always someone worse off than you – but these kids were not worse off – they were doing well and thriving because they had support and resources and a belief in themselves. The experience of meeting these kids gave me a different perspective and an understanding that my disability did not have to define me.

The last night of the camp was always disco night. A DJ and the lighting set up was hired, and we all dressed up and danced the night away. The night was a fantastic way to celebrate with all of my new friends and to know that I was able to be part of the crowd. As a teenage girl, boys were one of the most important considerations.

Back in Broken Hill, I had crushes, but none of the boys showed the slightest interest in me. So, imagine how excited I was when I was asked by several of the boys to dance. This was another first that I had never experienced before: dancing with a boy. We had dance classes at school, and I was always the last person to be picked for a partner, so this experience was like a dream.

I happily danced with one of the boys, and he kissed me. Yes, my first kiss. I must admit it was not all that good, but when you have never been kissed before, you cannot be too choosy. He was not just any boy but one of the popular boys at the camp, so now I was in a movie. I was the popular girl getting kissed by the popular boy at the dance.

It was like a fairytale: the girl from the country who had travelled to the city all alone with no confidence or self-worth suddenly had a whole group of fun new friends, was popular, had been able to experience life doing things that she had never tried before and felt for the first time in her life that she was not the outsider; not the girl that was disabled; not the girl that was poor or did not have all the right clothes or styles; not the girl that was scared to talk or be noticed in fear of being teased or bullied. And that girl was me.

I was like a butterfly that had emerged from my cocoon and was learning to spread my wings and fly. I knew I had found my place with people that I could trust and really call friends, but I also knew I had to push myself back into that cocoon before I returned to school, as there was no way that this newfound confidence in myself was going to be accepted back in my 'real' world.

At the end of the week, it was time to go home and return to that life. I had an internal light that had been sparked, though. There was something now that I knew I could look forward to every six months: somewhere that I could be the person I wanted to be with no judgments. Best of all, everyone liked me, and I liked them back.

We were all given a contact list with the other campers' details on it, and we all pledged to stay in contact with our friends by mail or phone before the next camp. For those living in the Sydney metro area, regular catchups were arranged for days in the city, which was fantastic. Suddenly, I had 30 new friends and the strength to go home and fight my battles with a stronger resolve of self-awareness, even if I knew I could not show this publicly.

Our farewells were reminiscent of those of my sisters at the bus station. Lots of tears and hugs goodbye. I recall it was raining the afternoon we left each other after our first camp, and I kept on blaming my tears for being raindrops. I didn't fool anyone.

Before she departed with her parents, Renee introduced me and requested that I be able to stay with her family the next time I flew over for a camp. They said they would be happy to have me stay, and we could work it out before the next camp happened.

Renee was a power in herself, and when she made up her mind, you knew that this was the outcome, so now, I had a place to stay every time I attended camps. Renee and her parents would pick me up from the airport on a Friday afternoon and take me back to the airport on the following Sunday.

Renee and I had a tradition of getting dropped off at the local shopping centre on the Saturday morning after camp finished, where we would submit our photo films for processing. We would both request double prints and then swap over our photos to have many memories to keep from our experiences.

Even walking around the shopping centre while waiting for the films to develop was exciting, fun, and a totally new experience. I had never been permitted to go shopping with my friends, even in Broken Hill, so having the trust of Renee's parents to go to the shopping centre alone was extraordinary.

I attended four more camps and a transition course before Grade Twelve and university, all staying with Renee and her family. Renee was a year behind me at school, so when I moved to Sydney, her parents took me under their wing, and I would spend most weekends at their home. I even spent my eighteenth birthday with her family.

I was so lucky to have people willing to extend their hospitality and kindness and treat me with love. Again, I had only ever seen this in books or movies, and now it was me. If this family had not extended its care, I would not have had the support to follow my dream of a positive future.

As I attended more camps, I realised that I wanted to live in Sydney in the future and that this was the place where I could be myself. Every time I had to go back to Broken Hill after a camp, I knew now that I had something to aim for, and no matter what the kids did and said to me at school, it was not the truth, and I had people who really liked and cared for me. My school friends had dreams for the future, and now I had some too.

I realised that being a journalist with a disability was not the best option for me in terms of a career, and I discussed what the other options might be with my friends from camps. As many of them had been using adaptive technology on computers from a young age, many had plans to follow a career in technology, but this did not interest me enough to create a career.

Still, I used the resources that I saw others using to understand that there were supports out there and that technology was improving and making it easier to live with a disability. The influence of the social workers and the support they gave me to challenge myself and experience new things were also among the influences in my future career. I knew how much the social workers had helped me, so this opened the door to me helping others similarly.

The friends I made at these camps are still friends – those connections we built and the friendships and commonalities shared have lasted a lifetime. We all had that unique time when many of us had to overcome our demons. Whether that be the bullies at school, the parents who wanted to wrap us in cotton wool or that nasty little voice that is inside our head telling us that we were not good enough and our disability meant that we would never be able to reach our dreams of a successful life.

Those weeks where I could escape my everyday life with the friends who taught me that I had value and the experiences I could participate in, were all things that literally changed my life.

When times got tough in Broken Hill, I had camp and my Sydney friends as an escape. I knew there was a possibility of a better life out there, and even though the path was not always easy to tread, once I had determined that Sydney was my future destination, the rest was just a means of reaching that goal.

Death

The shrill ringing of the telephone disrupted a peaceful Sunday morning, jolting me from the comforting embrace of sleep. Early Sunday phone calls rarely bring good news. The inconvenience is twofold when the phone is an ancient fixture on the hallway wall.

The only action was reluctantly dragging myself out of bed to answer it. No one else seemed willing to rescue me from this unwelcome task, so with a yawn and a rubbing of sleep from my eyes, I stumbled to the phone.

My mother was on the other end of the phone call. She had ventured off to Mildura for a girl's weekend away with her friends and was calling to check in on home and speak to my father.

I couldn't help but grumble about being abruptly awakened, pointing out that it was the daylight savings changeover. At 8am on a Sunday, any sensible fifteen-year-old would still be asleep and I asked why she was calling so early.

Despite my protest, my mother again requested to speak to Dad, who I assumed must have been outside in the yard. I checked the yard from the back door and could not see him. Maybe, to be honest, I did not even look that hard as it always takes me a while to wake up in the mornings and searching him out seemed like hard work.

Mindful that long-distance phone calls were costly, I sprinted back to the phone advising that I could not locate him, and my mother said that it was okay and that she would call that evening. She and her friends would do some tourist activities for the day and would be touring around the area.

Whenever my mother embarked on one of her weekend getaways with friends, it marked a particular time for Dad and me. Those were the moments when the grip of routine loosened, and we could enjoy the luxury of relaxation. It was a golden opportunity to strengthen our bond, free from the usual constraints of chores and routines.

Dad and I would engage in leisurely conversations that spanned many topics, accompanied by indulging in our favourite foods – the ones my mother disliked. While we never ventured into exotic cuisines, dishes like fish or slightly more adventurous fare than my mother's staple country meals graced our dinner table during those solo parenting weekends.

The house echoed with my favourite music, unapologetically played at a volume that would have drawn disapproving glances from my mother. The household sound system, a far cry from my modest portable cassette recorder, became the stage for my musical indulgence. I could sing and dance around and feel that I had no one judging me.

Dad was open to any style of music, and by this age, he let me use the car stereo with my musical choice as well. At this particular time, I was in my phase of loving *The Beatles*, which he also enjoyed, so he encouraged a mini dance party in the house.

Amidst the freedom, I still carried the responsibility of completing the standard household chores. Yet, there was a newfound sense of time and flexibility. These chores seamlessly intertwined with the activities I genuinely enjoyed, balancing duties and personal pleasures during those precious weekends of shared solitude with Dad.

This particular weekend, my mother left on Friday afternoon to go on the trip away. Dad took me to purchase some new music books on Friday after school, and I spent much of Saturday practising my music and doing the lessons in the new books.

Saturday afternoon, we went to the supermarket to choose something yummy to cook for dinner. We decided on my favourite at the time: veal schnitzel. While preparing dinner, we chatted and had a small glass of wine together.

After enjoying our dinner and a long chat about everything and nothing, we did the evening dishes. Dad excused himself to bed, a habit deeply ingrained in his early-to-bed, early-to-rise philosophy. March in Broken Hill still offered significant heat during the daytime, making the early morning hours ideal for tackling chores before the sun reached its scorching peak.

Ours was never a family prone to overt displays of emotion or physical affection. As he passed by, heading to his bedroom, a simple "*Goodnight*" was exchanged; I acknowledged him and returned to watching the movie I had on.

I stayed awake into the early morning hours, watching music videos on television. There was no rigidity of bedtime, another rule that was ignored when my mother was away. As long as I did not have the TV at dance party volume, Dad was cool with me doing my own thing.

After the rude awakening way too early with the phone, I decided since I was already out of bed, I could make myself a much-needed coffee and also bring in the washing from the outside line that I had washed the day before. The day seemed like it was going to be a hot one, and I did not want to have to contend with the scorching sun later in the day. I assumed that once I had got the washing from the line and put it away, another day ahead of doing whatever I wanted seemed to be stretched out ahead of me.

In contrast to my occasional procrastination with putting away laundry, I resolved to tackle the task promptly on this particular day. The thought of having the washing sorted and stowed away without delay held an appeal, freeing me to dedicate the remainder of the day to my chosen activities and not having the unfinished chores bothering me.

I folded the clothes and took the pile for my parent's room last. I would generally just put the pile for each of my parents on the end of the bed, and they would sort it into the cupboards and drawers themselves. When I entered the room, I realised something was terribly wrong.

My father's early rising habits, a remnant perhaps from his experiences in the Second World War, were nothing out of the ordinary. The morning light often found him up and about at 5am, following the wartime mantra of early to rise and early to bed – a practice ingrained for survival.

However, as the clock neared 9am on this particular day, the usual scene was disrupted. He, who was typically an early bird, lingered in bed longer than expected. Sensing an anomaly, my instincts whispered that this departure from the routine wasn't right. The uncharacteristic delay in his rise raised an alarm.

My father carried a history of heart troubles, which included past treatments for heart attacks during my middle sister's childhood. The consistent use of heart medication in his daily routine was a sign of acknowledging the fragility of his health, yet it never seemed to hinder his day-to-day activities due to it being a long-term condition. There was an unspoken understanding that his heart could ultimately determine his fate, although that day always appeared distant on the horizon.

Despite this awareness, when I discovered him remaining in bed this morning, a slight hope whispered, *"Perhaps he is deeply asleep."*

I desperately wanted to believe this, though deep down, I knew I was wrong.

Faced with the foreboding implications, I turned to a tactic inspired by his wartime experiences: attempting to awaken him with words. The lingering echoes of possible post-traumatic stress disorder (PTSD) from his time in war, although never formally diagnosed, influenced our interactions.

We refrained from physically touching him when trying to rouse him, always opting for the safety of verbal awakenings. However, on that particular morning, my usual calls went unheard.

Panic began chipping away at my composed exterior. In a moment of rising desperation, I resorted to what any fifteen-year-old girl in distress might do – I reached out to my best friend for guidance.

I called Kirsty, who had just returned from church with her family. I explained the situation, always trying to remain composed and clearly relay the information of what was going on. Her father was in the background while we were talking. They advised me to call emergency services and that they would drive right over to my house.

We were always taught to respect emergency services and never prank call – it was only to be used in case of a real emergency. I recall standing at the phone in the hallway, calling 000, and being asked which service I required.

After telling them I needed an ambulance and being connected to the ambulance service, I reported what was happening; I had woken up and then found my father still in bed and assumed he may have died.

The whole time I was on the phone, this little voice told me that Dad would wake up and walk out of the room, and I would get into trouble for calling the emergency services unnecessarily.

Of course, this did not happen. I was not kept on the phone. They advised an ambulance was on its way and that it would be there soon, and then they hung up on me.

Not that they could have done anything, but the practice now would be to keep a fifteen-year-old on the phone talking while the ambulance was enroute, not just leaving me to my own devices.

Thinking very logically, I thought finding my cat Peppy would be a good idea. I put him in my room with my parents' pet cat, so they were out of the way of the ambulance people when they arrived.

I don't know what else I did in that time frame, as the day began to blur from that time onwards. I remember keeping calm and keeping myself busy while I waited. Being a small town, it took only a short time for the ambulance to arrive.

I showed the medics into the room where Dad was, and they confirmed that he had passed away.

It's intriguing how my subconscious has blocked much of that memory. The idea of finding him in bed remains in my recollection, but the actual image eludes my conscious mind. The intricate details of the bed cover's design are vivid, yet the scene of him lying there has slipped from my memory. It's as if my brain, as a protective mechanism, shields me from the emotion of that particular visual.

Similarly, the recollection of the medics delivering the news of his passing is absent. I think I knew the truth when I realised he was in bed, and I did not need to recall the specific confirmation.

The paramedics did their duties efficiently, summoning the police and other necessary authorities. By this point, I sensed I was experiencing shock, a detached state that enveloped me in a surreal fog. The police, recognising the need for space, guided me outside, where we settled in the front yard while they asked many questions.

Amidst this scene, a work colleague of my mother's, familiar with our address on the main street, happened to drive by. Witnessing the gathering of emergency services at our home and being aware of my mother's absence for the weekend, she stopped by to ensure everything was in order. I knew her both from my mother's workplace and as the mother of a schoolmate, and there she sat with me, a comforting presence until Kirsty and her father arrived.

Some fragments of that day have blurred in my memory, but amidst the haze, one image stands starkly clear – the black dress adorned with white daisy-like flowers worn by my mother's workmate. She had been driving a taxi when she passed by.

Upon the arrival of Kirsty and her father, she departed, leaving me in the support of my friends and the police. Once I had recounted the events leading up to the discovery of my father and the subsequent call to emergency services, the conversation pivoted to discussing the logistics of locating my mother and notifying the family – an unusual predicament for them, contending with a fifteen-year-old without overseeing adults except for Kirsty's father.

I informed them that my mother was engaged in tourist activities in Mildura. The challenge lay in her unpredictable whereabouts, with no concrete plans or means of instant communication in the era before mobile phones. I provided the details of her lodging, a fixed point in the uncertainty of her schedule.

It was now a waiting game, relying on the hope that she would resurface where they could reach her sooner rather than later. I was informed that the police in Mildura would take on this task.

The policeman was probably beginning to wonder what to do with me.

"Who else can we contact?" he questioned.

My aunt resided in town but without a phone connection. The police opted to personally inform her about the unfolding circumstances, hoping she could provide support during this difficult time. Simultaneously, they emphasized my need to reach out to my siblings, each living away from Broken Hill. Confronting the inevitable task, I decided to get the calls underway.

My mother's first marriage had blessed her with two children considerably older than me, the eldest being my half-sister who we'd stayed with after the fire. But she'd since moved to Adelaide, so the first call in the sequence of notifying family fell upon my half-brother in Sydney. As I dialled his number, I steeled myself for the difficult conversation ahead. Strangely, the distance afforded by the telephone allowed me to recount the events with a measured reserve, sparing myself from the overwhelming surge of emotion that lurked beneath the surface.

His reaction on the other end of the line mirrored my own shock and surprise. He assured me he would arrange to travel out to Broken Hill as swiftly as possible. Despite the geographical gap, my half-brother had frequently transitioned between Sydney and Broken Hill throughout his adult life. The bond he shared with my father ran deep, a connection underscored by the fact that he had named his son after him. This phone call seemed to go reasonably well given the circumstances. Still, it was only the beginning, and I knew the task would get more complex.

My sisters – scattered across Adelaide – loomed as my next point of contact. My half-sister and middle sister shared a house, making it logical to reach them together. Aware of their additional phone handset, I requested they both be on the line for the conversation when my half-sister answered. The call was a deviation from my usual habits that likely set off alarms for them. After all, their fifteen-year-old sister wasn't known for initiating long-distance calls, especially in the middle of a Sunday.

With a deep breath, I conveyed the heartbreaking news of Dad's passing. The weight of the revelation hit my middle sister with an unparalleled force. Among us siblings, her bond with him was the most intimate. Having been under his care throughout her formative years, she had experienced the constant presence of a father who took early retirement upon my birth. He had been a steadfast figure during her school milestones and, more recently, guiding her through the process of university applications and beginning her life as an adult living away from home.

The impact of his sudden absence left her in a state of hysterical grief.

On the other end, my half-sister, absorbing the shock and grappling with her own emotions, assured me they would return to Broken Hill as soon as possible before she abruptly hung up the phone. That was by far the worst of the conversations I had that day. My sister's grief was overwhelming, and I knew that this event was going to affect her more than any of the rest of us.

Before leaving Adelaide, my middle sister called her childhood friend, who lived as our neighbour before the house burned down and asked her to come and be with me. This girl arrived at my house, waiting around in preparation to support my sister when she arrived.

Now, just for one more phone call to my eldest sister. I tried several times, but she was not at home. I did not want to leave an answering machine message but had no choice but to ask her to return my call and only speak to me if someone else answered. Goodness only knows who she thought was answering the phone when she called back or why her little sister was even making phone calls to her on a Sunday afternoon. I decided to give her specific instructions to only speak with me, as by this time, there were so many people around the house that I was worried that she would call back and someone else would tell her what had happened.

My phone calls did not stop there. I also contacted the husbands of the other ladies my mother was travelling with for the weekend. These people were all family friends and appeared at my house to join the ever-growing crowd of people simply waiting.

With all the people that appeared at my house, the following hours were filled with making lots of cups of tea and coffee. No one knew what to do or say, it was a weird silence where the walls seemed to be squeezing us all together in our grief. Everyone wanted to be together for support, but no one knew what to do or say.

After a few hours, I tried reaching my eldest sister again. Her husband answered and advised they had just arrived home. I asked him to fetch her to the phone and remember hearing her bantering with him as she walked to the phone. They had hard floors, and I could hear her heels echoing on the floorboards as she walked. Every step brought her closer to the devastating news that awaited her.

Once she was on the line, I delivered the heart-wrenching news, the weight of each word falling in the hollow space between us. Her response mirrored that of my other siblings—she pledged to come to Broken Hill immediately. With this call, the circle of communication was complete, and everyone who needed to be informed had been reached. To my knowledge, the police still had not tracked down my mother, so the person who needed to know the most was still unaware that she was now a widow, but my role in the delivery of information was complete.

It felt as if my sisters from Adelaide had shattered the land speed record with their swift arrival in Broken Hill. The usual five-and-a-half-hour drive condensed into a remarkably shorter span. The urgency of their journey, however, couldn't reverse the irreversible, and the reality of Dad's passing was not changed by their speedy arrival.

In truth, there was nothing anyone could do to bring him back. My sisters added to the people filling the house who had no idea what to do next. My middle sister locked herself away in our spare bedroom to suffer her grief in isolation. This is where she spent much of her time over the following days.

With the arrival of more family, Kirsty took the opportunity to call her father and request to be taken home as it was getting late in the day. In the years since, I have spoken to Kirsty about this day from her perspective., and she recounted that my dad was the first deceased person she had ever seen.

Still, he just looked like he was asleep. She felt sympathy for me but was uncertain how to help and give support. Her being there and supporting me through making all the phone calls and trying to keep me occupied was more than I could have ever requested. She promised that she would inform our friends of what had happened and also notify the teachers at school the following day, as I would not be going to school for a while.

I am so grateful for the friendship and support of Kirsty on this day and appreciate the vital role she played. Without her support, I would have been alone. Many people were around, but none of them with whom I was emotionally connected. The only people other than my dad that I really ever bonded with were my friends, and so having one of them to support me when all that I loved had been taken away was crucial and enabled me to deal with this situation better than I would have on my own.

By late afternoon, the police had successfully located my mother in Mildura, and she began the long journey back. The three-hour drive from Mildura to Broken Hill felt like a never-ending road to hell. She recollected to me in a conversation one day that she initially did not even want to return, stating that there was nothing left there for her. This was, of course, her shock taking hold, and it was not until one of her friends reminded her that I was there that she realised she did need to return.

On her arrival home, I sought solace in familiar tasks. Unpacking the car, laden with luggage and other items from travel, our friends' husbands were present, ready to provide support and transport them home. Meanwhile, my half-sister took charge, accompanying my mother to the hospital.

For her, facing the reality of my father's passing required a logical encounter at the morgue, a necessary step in comprehending the irreversible truth. I think they showed her through the little window like you see on television. It was decided that there was no autopsy required as he was on regular medications for his heart and had recently seen the family GP, who could confirm he had a heart condition.

Like I was on autopilot, just going through the motions and trying to keep myself busy with the responsibilities that I took on. No time for grief when you have a task to complete.

Eventually, everyone left the house and only my mother and two sisters remained. My eldest sister and her husband rented a motel room locally as there was no spare room for them at the house, and my half-brother had not yet reached us from Sydney, which was a ten-hour drive.

The days that followed seemed like an endless stream of visitors to the house. People coming to visit, flowers being delivered, the phone constantly ringing with people checking in and funeral arrangements to be made. Again, this was all a great distraction. I became the chief coffee and tea maker and played hostess to all the people who visited.

If there was another flower delivery or visitor, no worries; I took care of it. I even had a notebook with all the phone messages and flower deliveries noted. I knew we would want to thank these people later.

A meeting took place with representatives from the local *Returned Servicemen's League* to discuss funding for the funeral. Unfortunately, they decided against providing full financial support since my father's cause of death wasn't directly linked to his war service. The implications of this decision weighed heavily on my mother, introducing an additional layer of stress to an already challenging situation.

I recall assisting with the subsequent payments to the funeral home. This suggests that a payment plan must have been arranged, underscoring the financial strain my mother faced. Despite the inevitability of death, the notion of planning for such circumstances had never been a part of my parents' financial strategy.

On the funeral day, I was engrossed in choosing the perfect outfit. At fifteen, appearances held significance, and perhaps, in retrospect, this focus on selecting the ideal outfit distracted me from the reality of the event I was about to attend. The mantra felt simple: get ready, look your best and do what is expected.

As I took my seat at the front of the crowded chapel in the funeral home, I surveyed the faces around me. It struck me that my dad had been a remarkably popular man. His early retirement allowed him to use his time to help others and forge connections with numerous individuals who showed genuine affection and respect for him.

It was my first experience attending a funeral. When my grandmother passed away when I was eight, I was deemed too young to attend her funeral. This occasion marked my initiation into the solemn rituals of farewell. I promised myself that day that I would only ever go to a funeral for people that I genuinely cared for. This was not a place to go out of obligation; it was something to attend with actual care and respect.

The details of the service remain blurred in my memory. Still, I distinctly recall the packed chapel and the overwhelming sense of my dad's widespread impact. There was a viewing before the service, a moment my mother sought to say her goodbyes by touching my father.

I, however, chose not to attend. The memory of seeing him lying in bed after his passing had already been mercifully blocked by my brain, and I had no intention of forcing a recollection. I preferred to preserve my memories of him alive and vibrant, finding the concept of the viewing somewhat unsettling and, in my young mind, a touch morbid.

He probably never fully regained excellent health after the house burned down, the added stress taking its toll. However, I distinctly recall my father wanting to depart swiftly, preferably in his sleep.

In hindsight, I suppose that was one silver lining. He wasn't the type of man who would have coped well with a prolonged, debilitating illness. Just days before his passing, he was still on a friend's roof, diligently fixing gutters. This image encapsulates his enduring spirit and character.

Following the funeral, my friends joined me at our house, offering a respite from the sombre atmosphere filled with family and others who had gathered. Away from the formalities and obligations that defined the day, we found solace on my trampoline, away from the others who had gathered at my house. We shared stories of my dad, reminiscing about the memories we all cherished of him. Once again, the unwavering support of my friends became a vital anchor, helping me navigate the emotions that accompanied this day.

The funeral itself had followed a series of protocols and procedures. As part of the immediate family, specific responsibilities provided a structured focus, sparing me from dwelling too deeply on the gravity of the situation. However, during those candid moments on the trampoline, the weight of my father's absence truly sank in. The realisation hit me—my dad was truly gone, and the path ahead promised to be different and, in many ways, more challenging.

As the day unfolded, I understood that soon everyone would disperse, returning to their separate lives. I would be left to navigate the return to school, the routines of life, and all the mundane activities, now missing the one person who had been a constant presence every step of the way.

My relationship with my mother had never been particularly close or emotional. Despite sharing the grief over my father's passing, I foresaw that the coming months would be a formidable challenge. We were confronted with the task of navigating the responsibilities my dad had handled, all while grappling with our own grief and emotions. Deepest of all, we faced the intricate task of managing our evolving relationship with each other in his absence.

Fiona abseiling while attending blind camp

Fiona and her mother

Fiona as a toddler with her father in the backyard

Fiona in front of her school on graduation day

Fiona ready for her Year 12 formal

Fiona at home

Fiona and her parents at her christening

Location of Fiona's house site after the fire

Fiona standing on the red dirt in Broken Hill

Fiona sky diving

A photo of Fiona's teacher, Mr. Mason

Fiona with Peppy

A newspaper article about the house fire

Depression

Panic attacks: We hear about them often in our modern society, treating them as a standard part of overcoming some of what our subconscious brain is doing to protect our mental health. In the early 1990s, a teenage girl from the outback was never going to be diagnosed with this condition.

Was there something wrong in my brain? Did anyone really bother to ask, investigate, or even care? To be honest, I thought it was the latter.

The morning after Dad died, I added excitement to the already stressful circumstances. I was doing chores to keep some kind of routine and distraction and cut my finger on the cat food can. I have never handled seeing my own blood gracefully – especially from places it should not come from – and the cut on my finger was enough to make me feel faint. I had fainted before from the sight of blood, so I knew that I needed to put my head low to get the blood to run back that way.

In a blink, I found myself on the kitchen floor, my sisters hovering over me. I heard my mother on the phone to the emergency services. We had gone from never calling an ambulance to twice in the span of two days. I felt fine and wondered what all the fuss was. I wanted to get past the commotion and move on with my day.

Time seemed to stretch endlessly as we awaited the arrival of the ambulance – a paradox, considering the hospital lay a mere block away. In retrospect, I could have reached its doors faster on foot.

Despite my insistence, I remained confined to the kitchen floor where I had fallen. My fainting spell had been accompanied by some kind of seizure, which caused my family to panic and assume that there was more to the event than me simply having fainted.

I was accompanied in the ambulance to the hospital by my half-sister, after a thorough examination medical staff came to the conclusion that my mini seizure was most likely to be a stress reaction.

After a few hours of observation under the sterile hospital lights, I was discharged with a follow-up appointment recommended by my general practitioner. Surprisingly, there was no mention of seeking support from a counsellor or psychologist to navigate the emotional aftermath of the preceding day. The medical realm addressed the physical symptoms but left the emotional landscape unexplored.

In the aftermath of loss, everything must return to a rhythm and a new semblance of routine and normality. My siblings all went back to their lives, no doubt, to grapple with their own grief and to navigate the void that results from the loss of a parent. I was left with my mother to create a new life.

Historically, my relationship with my mother had never been close, possibly because she was not the primary caregiver. At this time, I was fervently pursuing independence, endeavouring to carve out an individual identity. Such pursuits inevitably spawned conflicts, a common rite of passage for teenagers seeking autonomy within their family dynamics, often clashing with the authority figure.

In our household, that role unequivocally belonged to my mother. With his seasoned approach, my father had discerned which battles to engage in and when to let things slide. His approach fostered mutual respect, encouraging open communication in both directions. His guidance took the shape of advice rather than directives, yielding more positive outcomes.

Now, thrust into a realm of solo parenting dominated by my mother, I struggled with the adjustment. Conversations with my sisters hinted at a mellowing in my mother's demeanour after my dad's passing, suggesting that I may have been granted more leeway and concessions to pursue my individual interests than my sisters had experienced at the same age. Yet, my yearning persisted for a different kind of relationship characterised by more significant support, interest, flexibility and empathy.

Broken Hill had a limited variety of opportunities for recreational activities targeted towards teenagers. During the scorching summer months, the pastime for most was congregating at one of the local swimming pools. However, the absence of swimming lessons and being extremely prone to sunburn made this option unavailable to me.

As we reached our mid-teens, a prevailing pattern among my peers emerged – venturing into the realm of local hotels. The allure lay in the lax enforcement of age restrictions on drinking, providing a social haven, especially for those with older friends of legal age.

Alternatively, popular kids often hosted parties at their homes – the details of which remained a mystery to me – as invitations were never extended my way. Despite my exclusion, the Monday after each weekend bore witness to a mosaic of stories detailing the highlights of these elusive gatherings.

Broken Hill wasn't immune to the familiar trifecta of underage drinking, drug use, and teenage pregnancy. Yet, my group of friends managed to sidestep these pitfalls. Whether due to our lack of invitations or a deliberate choice to focus on other pursuits, we remained on the fringes of such activities, observing the tales that circulated without becoming integral players in the narrative.

A week after that pivotal Sunday, it was time to return to school. Part of me was relieved to go back to following a structured routine and be distracted from what was happening at home.

That first week back was very surreal. My mother was still on leave from work, so she assumed the responsibility of dropping me off and picking me up from school. I felt that everyone was looking at me and gossiping. My friends became pillars of support, and I received incredible kindness from my teachers in those first challenging weeks. Many people, unsure of how to broach the subject, faltered in conversations about my father's passing.

Speaking with someone who has recently lost a family member is inherently challenging, a reality that even adults grapple with. Despite the outpouring of sympathy, the absence of a structured support system at school became apparent. There existed an unspoken expectation that I would swiftly return to my former self. This notion overlooked the intricacies of grief and the enduring impact of loss.

One of the initial challenges that surfaced was my mother's unreliability as a transportation resource for school. Despite waking her up with ample time for preparation and commuting, there was a recurrent issue. Whether she was oblivious to the time, indifferent, or if there were other factors at play, I often found myself missing the bell for homeroom and arriving late – typically ten or fifteen minutes behind schedule.

While this delay may seem minor, it necessitated obtaining a late pass and delivering it to the office after receiving the required signature. Consequently, I would miss the opening segment of my first class. This recurring scenario transpired at least two or three times each week. The frequency of these tardy arrivals should have raised concerns among those responsible for my well-being. It remains a mystery why no one seemed to catch on or inquire about the underlying reasons. Instead, the issue was allowed to slide, placing the onus on me to navigate and manage the situation independently.

Walking into class late is never a good thing. All eyes fall upon you, and you are the focus of all the other students while you take your place and get yourself ready. Add this to the fact that I was already unpopular at best and, at worst, the kid that everyone would take every opportunity to tease, bully or make uncomfortable; this drawing attention to myself was humiliating. It's pretty hard to be invisible when you are late to class *and* the unintentional centre of attention.

I explored alternative transportation options for school, especially after my mother resumed work. One solution involved walking approximately fifteen minutes to the nearest bus stop and then catching the school bus for the remaining journey. This became a viable choice on some occasions.

Other times, I simply opted to walk the forty minutes directly to school. For some individuals, this might have posed little of a challenge or, at most, been inconvenient. However, given the gradual loss of my vision as I grew older, navigating the route to and from school independently proved genuinely tricky and unsafe.

This difficulty was exacerbated by the extreme weather conditions in Broken Hill. The scorching summer days frequently saw temperatures soar above 40°C – while winter mornings often dipped below freezing. Navigating these conditions during my solo commutes, especially on rainy days, could have been better. Despite the challenges, it was a compromise I deemed necessary to avoid the recurring issue of being consistently late.

My father had been the love of my mother's life, and I understood she was grieving for herself. In the aftermath, the void he left behind included numerous chores he used to manage during the day while at home. Balancing these tasks with my mother's work commitments and my own school responsibilities became a complex juggling act.

As a result, I was handed a list of duties to complete between returning from school and her arrival home several hours later, intensifying the pressures I was already grappling with.

The restrictions imposed on my time robbed me of the freedoms enjoyed by kids my age. There was no room for after-school activities, socialising with friends, or even dedicating time to music practice or homework. Instead, my afternoons were monopolised by household chores – tending to pets, handling laundry, housekeeping, and preparing dinner. While I acknowledge the valuable life skills I developed during this period, managing the day-to-day affairs of the household became an overwhelming responsibility.

Upon returning home, my mother contributed to a few tasks and supervised weekend chores to some extent. However, it felt like my role shifted from a participant in a family to a live-in maid, shouldering the responsibilities my father once managed. If my relationship with my mother was strained before, this period exacerbated our dynamic. While we didn't engage in shouting matches or arguments, I felt akin to *Cinderella* – devoid of choice, compelled to fulfil assigned tasks without much say.

Let me clarify: it wasn't always a gloomy atmosphere. Occasionally, I sensed my mother's loneliness or her longing for Dad, prompting her to engage in conversations with me. While these exchanges were never deep or emotionally charged, there were moments when we connected on a superficial level. The topics rarely delved into my personal life but revolved around daily household affairs or current events.

Moreover, there were instances where I enjoyed flexibility, allowing me to visit with my friends during the initial months after Dad's passing. These moments became crucial lifelines, providing a reprieve and helping me endure the challenges of that period.

There were also plenty of dark times. At home, I would hide in my bedroom and cry for hours. I felt such a sense of loss. My hero and the person I truly loved had been taken away. Without a chance to say goodbye or tell him how much I loved him.

I had times when the grief was so overwhelming, I was in a black pit of despair. Nothing seemed like it would ever be right again. I hated myself and hated my life. I could not see any point in the future as I felt there was nothing worthwhile to pursue.

The only person who really cared and supported me was gone, and now I had nothing. Even my friends were at a loss as to how to help me. Of course, that's not a skill most fifteen-year-olds know: how to support a friend through grief. They did their best, and there were times when this was enough, but at other times, I was inconsolable.

My school days drifted by in a hazy blur. I navigated my way through classes as a distraction. Still, during breaks, mainly when my friends were engaged in other activities, I often found myself secluded in the girls' bathrooms, tears streaming down my face. The school bathrooms, however, were far from a private sanctuary – they lacked the safety of solitude. Anyone entering could easily discern the presence of someone behind a closed stall. If I made a sound; it became apparent that I was in distress. There was no refuge, no safe space, and no one to confide in who understood what I was going through.

It was a recipe for disaster just waiting to happen.

The panic attacks persisted, disrupting my daily life. On two occasions at school, the intensity of a panic attack forced me to be sent home. This situation interrupted my mother's workday, as there was no alternative arrangement for my transportation. I recall when she picked me up from school in her taxi, dropped me home, and promptly returned to work. I appeared outwardly fine to her, and the imperative of earning income overshadowed the need to check in on me.

Whenever I encountered stress beyond the overwhelming load that had become my norm, my brain would react, triggering yet another panic attack. The cycle perpetuated, leaving me caught in the relentless grip of anxiety along with my overwhelming sadness.

An ever-increasing spiral of despair enveloped my existence, steadily intensifying with each passing day. The hatred for my current life grew within me, fostering an urgent desire to escape through any available means. The burden of detesting the monotonous chores and the drive to excel in school – where failure was inconceivable in my mind – created an inescapable web of pressure that seemed to originate from every conceivable angle. The weight of expectations bore down on me with an ever-increasing force.

During the second episode of a major panic attack at school, my mental state must have been severely compromised, prompting the school to call for an ambulance. This incident unfolded during Sports Day – a typically stressful occasion for me, given my disability often prevented active participation.

I recall the sweltering heat and the outdoor setting on the school oval. Still, my recollection is blurred as to what triggering event propelled me into a full-blown panic attack. Kirsty was by my side, and the teacher sought the assistance of the deputy principal, indicating the severity of the situation. I vividly recall being carried across the school grounds by the deputy principal, drawing considerable attention and fuelling the gossip mill.

Kirsty accompanied me to the hospital in the ambulance. She later recounted that the ambulance driver, unfamiliar with the route from our school to the hospital, struggled with navigation. This was before the advent of GPS. Navigating Broken Hill was straightforward, especially along the main road for most of the journey. Fortunately, Kirsty provided accurate directions, swiftly bringing us to the hospital.

Upon arrival, I found myself in the Accident and Emergency department, where, to my dismay, they opted to cut off my clothes for the purpose of attaching heart monitors and conducting an examination. It proved to be a thoroughly embarrassing experience, exacerbated by the destroyed attire being my best sports uniform.

Following this particular incident, I found myself admitted to the hospital for overnight observation. I recall my mother eventually arriving at the hospital, her whereabouts during my crisis unknown, a recurring theme throughout that year. There was no discussion regarding the reason for my hospitalisation, and the medical staff solely concentrated on potential physical issues rather than mental concerns.

Upon my discharge the next day, a staff member suggested that considering the challenges of the past few months, I might benefit from counselling. Regrettably, this recommendation was never pursued further.

Back to school, back to the routine of helplessness, and now I had another thing to add to the list of weirdness; I was the girl who was carried to the office by the school principal and then got taken away in an ambulance.

Reflecting now with the clarity of hindsight, I perceive a certain neglect in the lack of support or check-ins that were put in place for me. Mental health management was not within the scope of the school system during that era, and it was evident that the healthcare system lacked the knowledge or resources to proactively ensure my safety.

In reality, I was far from safe. From a mental health standpoint, I was in disarray, akin to a ticking time bomb, poised to explode at any moment.

During this challenging period, my misery was compounded by the onset of migraine headaches – a hereditary issue in our family. Triggered by hormones, stress and a decline in my eyesight, these migraines plagued me regularly, typically striking at least once a week, with Monday afternoons being the usual time. The experience of walking home under the scorching sun, carrying my heavy school bag – while feeling ready to throw up any moment – was nothing short of unbearable.

Unfortunately, I never received any medical assessment or diagnosis for these migraines. Consequently, my only recourse was relying on basic pain medication and seeking refuge in a dark room. Attempting to alleviate the excruciating pain with a dose of medication followed by a brief rest generally proved ineffective.

If you have ever tried to get rid of a migraine headache by taking a *Panadol* and then lying down for ten minutes before doing your chores, you'd know that this is not an effective method of pain management.

Despite my mother also experiencing migraine headaches, her ability to provide assistance was limited. Her focus was entirely dedicated to work and maintaining control over her life, leaving little time or energy for her to support me in navigating this debilitating condition.

Upon introspection, I recognise a correlation between substantial vision loss and periods of heightened stress. While this connection might lack scientific validation, personally, I can pinpoint instances in my life marked by significant stress events, coinciding with notable progression in my vision deterioration. I noticed myself beginning to struggle with reading standard print sizes, necessitating the enlargement of my school materials when photocopied. Receiving handouts on A3-sized pages instead of the typical A4 format became another means by which my disability became conspicuous to all my classmates.

The attempts to discreetly fold my page in half to avoid notice proved futile, as others inevitably observed and took the opportunity to comment. Once again, my disability seemed thrust into the spotlight, intensifying my self-consciousness.

This obvious loss of my visual acuity also pushed home the concept that I was in fact going blind. It is easy to ignore when the deterioration is gradual, however when something substantial changes like the need to use large print, the inevitable is hard to ignore.

The most heart-wrenching aspect of losing my ability to read standard print was the inability to seek refuge within the pages of a book. This sanctuary had allowed me to escape from reality.

Throughout my life, I cherished the solace found in reading, but suddenly, I found myself dependent on audiobooks. In the early 90s, audiobooks were far from mainstream. Armed with a bright blue cassette player adorned with oversized, brightly coloured buttons, I faced limitations – no headphone jack and only a mains power plug port.

A typical novel spanned twelve cassettes, recorded at half speed and dual tracks. This restricted me to reading solely at home, where I had access to the bag of tapes and a power source. The range of books available to me was also constrained, leaving me unable to enjoy the latest bestsellers or even those tailored for my age group.

The frustration of waiting for new books dispatched through the post from *Vision Australia* in Sydney added to my sense of confinement. Deprived of the option to lose myself in a book at the school library during breaks or wherever I happened to be, I found myself with ample time for introspection, contemplating life, and its challenges.

As my vision continued to decline, my attention shifted to all the activities I could no longer engage in. The prospect of the future appeared bleak. My aspirations and dreams had always assumed a level of eyesight that would afford me some degree of independence. Given my already fragile mental health, my thoughts were overwhelmingly pessimistic, focusing on the seemingly insurmountable challenges that lay ahead. I would steadfastly concentrate on all the things that I could not do and seemed impossible.

There was no respite from the shadows of my dark thoughts, and it felt like no one was capable or willing to lend a helping hand. In this mental state, everything appeared distorted and out of proportion. While, in reality, there were people who cared, I couldn't perceive their support. I felt isolated, convinced that nobody truly understood the challenges of my life. Despite yearning for support, it never materialised. It seemed I had no alternative but to persist in my current struggle, holding on by the thinnest of threads.

It felt like my absence from the world would go unnoticed, and the idea of escaping the daily agony by ending my life became a compelling option. I reached a point of profound darkness where suicide seemed like the only way out. However, my desperation was matched by a sense of helplessness. Even in contemplating suicide, I couldn't devise a foolproof plan that would ensure the outcome I desired.

Unable to drive, a purposeful car accident was out of the question. Access to a firearm was non-existent. Even thoughts of self-harm were met with physical limitations – I would faint before causing any significant harm. The lack of access to drugs or medications added another layer of frustration, knowing that such attempts often proved unsuccessful. Ideas like train tracks or road accidents were dismissed due to the potential impact on others.

The burden I carried grew heavier as I not only grappled with the desire to end my life but also struggled to find a method that felt conclusive. Despite having a few friends, their connections extended beyond me, making it seem like my absence wouldn't be deeply felt.

My family, scattered geographically and emotionally distant, added to the belief that my departure would likely go unnoticed. Thus, the only remaining barrier to my decision was the uncertainty of how to exit this life.

The days dragged on, and while everyone around me was embracing the typical teenage experiences, I felt trapped in a cycle of sorrow and isolation. It seemed as though no one truly listened or comprehended the depth of my struggles, intensifying my sense of loneliness. Even when my school friends or those I met at blind camps in Sydney reached out, the connection felt fleeting, and soon enough, the dark curtain of despair descended, enveloping me once again.

During this period, I grappled not only with the loss of my dad but also with the realisation that I needed to contemplate my post-high school future. It became evident that my dream of becoming a journalist was unattainable, and I had to explore alternative career options. Knowing I couldn't remain in Broken Hill after graduation due to the lack of opportunities, I faced a time when envisioning a future for myself seemed nearly impossible – pun intended.

The challenges brought about by my diminishing vision and persistent migraine headaches made my physical existence a constant struggle. School remained an uncomfortable environment, and the weight of managing the household responsibilities at home continued to rest squarely on my shoulders. The convergence of these difficulties painted a picture of a life characterised by physical hardships and deteriorating mental health.

I won't delve into specifics, but there were moments where I made attempts to end my life or had near misses. Since there was never anyone present to witness, I managed to crawl away from those situations unnoticed, no one the wiser to what had occurred.

I had developed an effective facade that convinced people I was okay. Most of the time, I operated under the radar, never being questioned about what was happening. When there's minimal emotional connection between individuals from the start, the impact of depression can be concealed or, at the very least, go unnoticed – especially during those times when mental health was something never openly discussed.

The remainder of the year and my sixteenth year were primarily characterised by a state of either numbness, periods of depression, or, at times, a deliberate performance to convince both myself and those around me that everything was okay.

Big Sister Returns

About six months after Dad's passing, I was given news that I found impossible to comprehend. My middle sister made an unexpected announcement: Due to a twist of fate, she declared she intended to return to Broken Hill to live in our family home.

A devastating revelation: I would lose my cherished independence. I dreaded the thought of having a watchful eye over me.

Someone who would check in and check up on me incessantly, disrupting my routine. Six years my senior, my sister and I had that underlying annoyance that sisters have for each other at times. I feared this would be like when we had lived at home together before she departed for university. Back then, we had shared a bedroom, another added layer to the irritation we often felt.

She had her moments of kindness and caring, but in the past, her older sister's perspective painted me as the pesky little sibling perpetually in her way. Recollections of our having an imaginary demarcation line in our room and that we were not supposed to pass into each other's territories resurfaced. Her stuff was hers, and mine was mine. I was always really messy, providing endless frustration. Such a contrast, her order clashing with my chaos.

I always wanted to borrow her stuff and listen in or spy on whatever she was doing and would constantly impinge on her personal space. If she was sitting on her bed immersed in reading a book or studying, I would be on my side of the room singing or dancing up a storm and making such a cacophony of noise that goodness only knows how she never erupted in anger with me.

Fortunately, this time we would not have to share a room. The house our family had moved into after the house fire granted us enough space to have a room each, and still one spare. This would still be too intimate for me, though, as across the hallway was very different from the 500 kilometres that had previously separated us.

My memories painted her as bossy and sometimes dismissive, which fuelled my apprehension about her return. I had meticulously crafted a system where my mother and I could live harmoniously for the most part, and suddenly, my sister's presence would disrupt the delicate balance.

I remember venting my frustrations to a girl at school about the bleak prospect of my sister returning home and how terrible this turn of events was for me. It was like another dark shadow looming over me.

We sat in the advanced math class, the only two girls among fifteen boys, so we would occasionally gravitate to each other for conversation. She tried to convince me that things would not be so bad, but I remained convinced that my big sister's return would spell disaster for me.

Selfishly, I had not taken much time or consideration of the reason why she was coming home. The factors were a secondary concern to the perceived impact it would have on me. I had not thought of what personal hardships brought her back. She also was still grieving my father; a loss that was still deeply affecting us all.

Moreover, she had to abandon her university studies before completing her degree. Her housemate decided abruptly that they were moving out and gave no notice and time for her to find a replacement. With her part-time job and university commitments, there was no way that she could afford to cover rent herself, so she had no option but to abandon her independent pursuits and move back home.

For anyone, this would have been a difficult situation. But for my sister, it meant relinquishing her academic dreams, freedom, and independence and returning to Broken Hill – a place with uncertain prospects. She had worked so hard to leave home and attend university; now, all in one fell swoop, it had all changed.

She was the brainy sister and the one known for her intellect and academic excellence. Her high school teachers still remembered her, often mentioning her when I was in their classes. She had obtained remarkable scores on her final high school exams and was thriving at university. Now, she had to bid farewell to that life and return to a place she had tried so hard to escape.

The devastation of the house fire had also devoured her cherished childhood possessions and a part of her developmental identity.

The fire had snatched away a world she had left, thinking it would remain intact for the future and had been reduced to ashes.

Selfishly, I had only considered the impact her return would have on me: little did I consider that her coming back would be one of the most significant situations of my life. A game changer and a blessing in disguise.

Building our relationship took time and patience. We discovered that, as we both grew older, the age gap that had caused such contention in the past no longer mattered so much. In fact, much to my surprise, my sister had become patient, understanding and empathetic. It was as though those years between our ages dissolved.

In some ways, she stepped into the traditional role of a big sister, offering advice, helping style my hair, and giving fashion tips. We would happily share clothes with each other and shop together, her teaching me how to make the best of limited resources. She also willingly shouldered a large proportion of the household responsibilities that I had taken on, allowing us both to enjoy the luxury of some personal time.

It was amazing to me how the chores that seemed so mundane done alone, were suddenly more interesting when shared. There were times when it did not feel as though we were doing something we disliked – my sister always managed to brighten up even the most difficult times with a smile or something funny.

The daily ritual and drama of transportation to school was solved when my sister became my go-to transport provider, ensuring

I got there safely and on time whenever she was not at work. It provided a huge relief and resolved my daily transportation worries. This gave me one less thing that I needed to worry about and removed stress from my life.

When relating to our mother, we became staunch allies; working together to navigate the quirks and challenges of her behaviours. We were never the type of sisters who shared deep, meaningful secrets, but we supported each other when needed. Our united front demonstrated to us that it was much better working as a team, looking out for each other and preventing situations that could cause conflict or create messy arguments that could have escalated in our living space.

At times, we indulged in adolescent mischief, devising creative ways to bypass curfews. Instead of using the noisy front gate when coming home late from being with friends, we opted for a stealthy leap over the fence. We justified it to our mother as an attempt to keep the noise down, but it was a clever strategy to avoid detection, and this small eccentricity also seemed amusing.

We thought ourselves quite brilliant – although who knows what passing motorists thought of our peculiar behaviour. It's lucky we never were reported to the local police as potential intruders and that the pet dog that lived in our front yard was too old and deaf to be a good guard dog. And witnessed our nocturnal adventures silently.

Another shared amusement was us renaming our mother's cat. I cannot recall the cat's original name, but it tended to meow loudly, so we christened him 'Jaws'. He obviously liked this name as soon he embraced it and began to respond only to that name, completely disregarding any other calls. Our mother was unamused by our nickname choice for her beloved pet, but it brought us endless amounts of amusement. Every time the cat unwittingly participated in our little game; we thought it particularly amusing.

My sister was also willing and able to assist me with schoolwork. The person to provide proofing and review of my assignments and offer general advice on managing my school life. This support proved invaluable during my final years of high school.

Generally, I did not ask for much support, but having her academic skill was helpful. She also noted when I was becoming overwhelmed by the pressure I had put upon myself to achieve and offered opportunities to relax or would take on some additional chores to free up my time.

She also provided the much-needed reassurance that the Grade Ten prom was less critical than I believed it to be. My sister assured me that the Grade Twelve formal would hold more significance and told me it would be a memorable night and she would help with what I needed when the time came.

She kept her promise by helping me find a suitable dress to borrow from our eldest sister to prepare for the event. She surprised me with matching earrings to the choker I had selected for the evening as a special surprise gift. Even though she was at work the night of the formal, she called to check in on me as I was getting ready and wished me a fantastic night.

My friends and I attended the formal together, this time JR and I, along with Kirsty and Peter. We had a truly amazing time, another one of those times when, even though I was still an outsider, I was included in the things that every other student does and takes as a rite of passage in life.

With the support of my sister and friends, this night was the end of an era and the dawning of me being ready to embark upon the next phase of my life. I was no longer as concerned about what others thought of me. The ridicule and the torment of the other students I had attended school with were in the past. My sister showed me, that after a few years, school people who were not your friends are no longer an important part of the story.

On the day I graduated high school, my sister was my cheerleader again. She braided my hair before heading to work so I would feel special and wished me the best of luck. Her high school experience had its own challenges, so she understood how much importance there was on the day that this chapter came to a close. She knew the hard work I had put in towards ensuring that I had, like her, reached my academic peak to enable me to achieve results that would give me options for the future.

For her, our parents had been present to celebrate her achievements; for me, she was the key support. I prohibited my mother from attending the graduation ceremony and opted to spend the day with my friends and their families. She had not been instrumental in my academic journey – unless you count disinterest or outright negativity – so it seemed hypocritical for her to attend and celebrate my hard-earned success.

My sister's added years had afforded her more opportunities to spend time and learn from our father. I missed the chance to have an adult conversation with Dad, but she would often generously share the wisdom and advice that he had imparted to her, which I may have received in due course had he still been with us.

I did not always heed her guidance at the time; as teenagers, we always think we know the best, but looking back, I am grateful for her care and support. It took me some years to truly appreciate and follow the valuable advice she had given me over that period. She helped to keep my mother at bay and fill the void left by losing our father.

To this day, my middle sister remains the closest member of my family, despite her living on another continent. The communication threads are stronger between us than with many other family members. Across the years, our bond remains strong. She had the unique experience of living with each of our siblings away from the family home – while I have only ever shared family living with her or our parents. The second time around was markedly better and exceeded my expectations.

My sister unknowingly was a significant role model for me. In the way she had navigated her own challenges and built inner strength and resilience, she showed me that I too could overcome the obstacles that I had in front of me. I often think that she was just doing her best with the limited resources she had at the time, still navigating her own struggles, but was instrumental in helping me through mine.

Although her presence did not miraculously resolve my struggles with depression, self-doubt, and self-dislike, she did show me that there were other possibilities in life and that good times could be part of the journey.

Through her indirect support, I gradually emerged from my darkest thoughts, and even though I continued to grapple with my mental health, I was no longer alone in the struggle. The teen drama had turned into a tale of growth, uncovered love, and respect; and an unbreakable bond between two sisters.

Oh, and if you've been wondering all this time that as she is the middle sister, is a baby sister going to appear? No, because although she has always been a middle sister to me, she is actually the middle *child*.

Growth After Grief

The weariness clung to every inch of my being as I endured the last lesson of the day in my Grade Eleven Legal Studies class. The minutes dragged on, each tick of the clock echoing my silent plea for the day to mercifully end. Exhaustion weighed heavy on my shoulders, and a pounding headache throbbed as a persistent reminder of the day's strain. The unforgiving heat outside only added to my misery, knowing that a long walk awaited me on the way home.

Our teacher always did his best to be engaging and teach us something interesting with a sprinkling of personal stories and examples to make the lessons more compelling and engaging. I did not want to engage that day and had a little nap at the back of the class – which seemed much more enjoyable. Imagine my horror when he began speaking of a major assessment:

"You will do a class presentation of around ten minutes on any legal topic of your choice."

If my afternoon had not been miserable already, this was the worst thing that could have happened, and now it has gone from bad to downright disastrous. The mere thought of giving a class presentation sent shivers down my spine. I was the kid who tried to keep a low profile.

The prospect of standing in front of the classroom with everyone's attention and scrutiny on me for one minute, let alone the dreaded ten, was like some kind of sacrificial torture. I had a healthy competition with the other two students vying for top honours in this subject. I was reluctant to let them get one up on me with this assessment. Still, there was no way I could ever pull this off and not end up the laughingstock of the class.

Assessment sheets with directions for the presentation were handed out. I discovered I had two weeks to prepare, and our names would be called randomly to present over the subsequent lessons. I figured I had little choice but to participate, so I needed to come up with some topic that I really knew the subject matter for and that I had some passion about so at least I would have my content sorted out and would get good marks for that segment even if the actual presentation was a hopeless disaster.

By this time, the really mean students had left school, and I was hoping there would be no overt judgement and name-calling or teasing while I was at the front of the class.

Please be kind, devil children, and do not make this worse than being thrust into the pits of hell.

Finally, the bell for the end of class and school rang, and it was time to escape. Lucky for me, one of the mature-age students from the class with whom I would sit offered me a ride home. He must have detected my misery and felt sorry for me. Either way, it solved the problem of walking home in the Broken Hill heat with a killer headache.

On our way home, we discussed the options for presentation topics. I told him I did not really care at that point in time as I felt like I was dead. He laughed and said, *"That is a good topic."*

Something sparked inside me, and I thought there may be something in that, but I filed it away for another time when I had more energy to focus.

With the time for the presentation drawing nearer, it was time to decide on the topic. My mind travelled back to the day I had been discussing the assessment with Allan on the way home, and we spoke about death being a good topic. I reflected a little on my personal circumstances over the previous year. I thought that speaking of teen suicide may be an interesting and potentially helpful topic.

Living in a rural area, none of us were unaffected by suicide of some kind. We had people from school or others in wider family social groups that had taken their lives. Suicide is a high-risk factor for teenagers, and often, it is the people that you think are managing best who are suffering silently.

Even though the other students in my class did not have any love for me, and I had no real connection with any of them, I thought this was a topic that was not only going to be of interest to me but something that I could speak on in front of others and maybe, who knows, one of my classmates may gain something from it too. I had a problem, though.

Where do you get information about this topic?

It was way before the internet was ever available. Schools and even the local library would have little recent data or information. There were not really many welfare agencies in Broken Hill that I could use as a resource to access information. I was a little stuck. I needed some help.

Mr. Mason was our Legal Studies teacher and also one of the deputy principals, so I thought that he may have had the answers I required. Knock, knock on his office door. Sat at his desk, he looked up, saw it was me, and gestured for me to come in.

"How can I help you?" he asked.

"I need to know about suicide," I said, slowly venturing my way into his office. I have never seen a man leap from his desk and look so worried.

"Please sit down," he gestured toward the chairs set up for student conferences at the other end of his office. *"Can I get you anything? Cup of tea?"*

What teenager wants a cup of tea?

Obviously, I had shocked him, and he was so flustered he had no idea what he was saying. Maybe he needed the cup of tea more to calm his nerves after that bomb I dropped.

After closing the door and coming to sit opposite me, he asked the most pivotal question of my life. I just did not know it at the time.

"Is this for you or someone else?"

Now, we had under 700 students at the school; added to that, I was in a class he taught as well, and he was the one who often signed off on my late passes. He knew all too well what emotional state I was in. I am not at all surprised that I may have been in a place where suicide was a reasonable consideration.

You can imagine his relief when I answered, "*Well, both, some for me, but mostly for others, and this is the topic I want to cover for the presentation.*"

He still looked slightly worried, but he could put his teacher persona back on and not worry about playing school counsellor or calling for help. And he did not have to worry about giving me more cups of tea.

For me, this moment was the time that I realised that my own experience gave me something that no one else had. My crappy life has shown me that no matter how bad things are, each day is another day. Even if that day turns out to be wrong, there is always tomorrow. My lived experiences of life and managing my obstacles allowed me to help others.

This is where my reptile brain snapped into place, and I decided I really had something to live for. That I had some kind of value, something to contribute. From here, I had a new goal. I was going to work out the best way to help other people, so they did not have to experience the trauma and depression that I had.

I told him that, to be honest, I had been feeling pretty miserable. Things were not so bad at that time, though, and I figured if this was me and my situation, there must be others who were feeling extreme pressure and may have also experienced dark thoughts.

He seemed quite impressed that I could look past my situation and offer suggestions for something that would help others. A sneaky thought to myself was that this was a bonus as it would give my presentation more credibility when he knew the background behind it.

Mr. Mason was happy to provide me with the resources I required. After his little mini-heart attack, handing me some documents and swooshing me out of his office was a priority. As the deputy in charge of student welfare, he had been recently provided with a folder of information covering the topic I was interested in.

It had some statistics, clear signs to build awareness, and valuable strategies to implement to support people. This was a fantastic information folder and gave me all the resources I required to assemble the most comprehensive presentation ever. I just hoped that the presentation skills match the content.

Soon, the day of the presentations arrived, and gladly, mine was one of the first names pulled out of the hat. Better to have it over and done with early on; that way, I could observe the others and know that my torture was complete. I stood up in front of my class and wrote the word 'SUICIDE' on the board in big capital letters.

Hopefully, this shocked some class members who were daydreaming into paying attention. I figured if I were going to do this, I would give it my best shot. After going through the suicide statistics, talking about the reasons why suicide prevention was so important and then speaking in general about mental health,

I presented the class with a list of risk factors and behaviours that they could watch out for in themselves and their friends.

Finally, I provided a handout of the local contact resources for anyone who needed additional help. That ten minutes seemed to take a lifetime, but it was bearable in some ways because I was doing something I cared about. It was something that had meaning to me and something that could make a positive change for someone else.

It was the best presentation I had ever provided at high school, and I was quite pleased with myself. It was hard to work out what the rest of the class thought. I was relieved to have it over and scampered back to my seat and out of the spotlight as soon as possible. Still, I knew I had averted a potential disaster.

A few weeks later, when we had been provided our results for the assessment, I was even more pleased. I managed to get the top mark for the presentation – outranking my two fierce competitors for marks in that subject. Both the content and the presentation skills elements had been well received. This also helped cement that the idea of doing something with my life and using my experience to help others had some validity.

Leap of Faith

Leap out of a perfectly good aeroplane? Sure, why not give it a go. What do I have to lose?

My friend JR encouraged me to enter a radio competition to win a free skydive. The company was coming in from Adelaide to promote their service and get some sign-ups from locals. Opportunities like this were unavailable in a country town like Broken Hill, so it was very unusual. The allure of winning this skydive was not merely the thrill of the experience but also the chance to break free from the ordinary confines of activities that Broken Hill had on offer.

The quest to win the skydive began by entering with a reason why the skydive was going to change your life. I figured that if I was going to go blind, this would be something fun and exciting to do while I still could see. Who wants to avoid seeing the ground coming up to meet them while flying through the air, hoping the parachute will open anyway?

So, my entry stated that I had grown up in Broken Hill and would love to follow my adventurous streak and have the opportunity to skydive before I went blind. I was in with a good chance, as many other contestants would say they wanted an adventure or thought it would be fun.

I had developed my sense of adventure from doing the activities on the blind camps. Those times were an opportunity to face my fears and the challenges of doing things that were sometimes scary but always fun in pushing my boundaries.

Reflecting on those moments of leaping off cliffs with nothing but a rope as a safety net, hurling oneself out of an aeroplane seemed like a logical progression.

As with many things in life, my entry into the competition lost focus and importance once submitted, receding into the background amongst the activities of my daily existence. That year, my commitment rested upon the demands of school life and focusing on the required outcomes. My results had the potential to shape or shatter my future dreams, so schoolwork was always at the forefront of my actions and thoughts.

One Monday morning, as I prepared for school amidst the haze of a miserable cold, the shrill ring of the telephone disrupted me from my zombie-like state. I felt so terrible that staying in bed at home from school seemed like a good option, but an assessment was set for that day, and I needed to attend.

Sniffling and nursing a sore throat, I wearily answered the phone, fervently hoping for a swift resolution; they would say whatever they wanted and let me go back to using my energy to get ready to leave the house for my school day ahead.

To my surprise, the radio announcer on the other end, radiating infectious enthusiasm even at that early hour, delivered news that momentarily made me forget my suffering.

"You've won the competition for a skydive!" he exclaimed with unbridled excitement, his words clearing the fog in my brain.

I mustered up a half-enthused, *"Okay,"* – although I'm sure that he was expecting a better response.

Usually, people scream, shout, or at least show some joy; I did not have it in me that morning. Undeterred, he told me we would air and announce me as the winner and ask why I had entered.

We went live on the radio in a mini interview. Of course, they wanted to promote the skydive as much as possible, and the blind girl as a winner was a feel-good way to start the day. I tried to sound enthusiastic, and sure I was. This would be a fantastic thing to do, and it seemed exciting and adventurous.

Sadly, I did not convey the excitement they hoped for. Still, at least it was an interesting story for the listeners, and now I had something exciting to do. As the radio segment concluded, I was instructed to be at the local airport for the skydive that approaching weekend. The gravity of the situation settled in, leaving me with little time to fathom the magnitude of what I had signed up for.

Amidst the whirlwind of emotions and the impending thrill of the unknown, I faced the dual challenge of overcoming a stubborn cold and preparing to plunge headfirst into an adventure that awaited me in the sky. I had taken on adventure at the blind camps, but this was on a different scale.

Upon reaching school, I eagerly shared the news of my impending skydive with my friends. The excitement radiated from JR, knowing I loved doing the adventure activities at camp. He thought this was an excellent opportunity for me to do something unusual, which would be fun for me in my 'normal' life, not just find adventure when I went to blind camps.

JR's enthusiasm mirrored my own anticipation, emphasising the prospect of this skydive as not just another escapade but a unique and thrilling experience to be undertaken. This skydive would also be something to prove that all of the people who underestimated my capacity due to my disability would be proven incorrect.

However, a minor hiccup presented itself in that, being under eighteen, I needed help to autonomously sign the indemnity insurance forms required for the skydive. After a lengthy discussion with my mother, and I believe some intervention from my sister, it was agreed that they would come along and sign the relevant documents while supporting my adventure.

JR also came to support me on the day. After all, that is what best friends do. He had his camera and a video camera borrowed from the school art department to capture the whole event for prosperity.

We arrived at the Broken Hill airport early on the Saturday morning. The day was a clear, sunny autumn day, and thankfully, I had gotten over my cold and felt much better. I was excited but also full of trepidation about how this would go. Despite the statistical realities of the dangers inherent in skydiving, I found myself surprisingly undaunted.

The thought of plummeting from the sky held no terror for me; after all, I had danced with the idea of meeting death on my own terms not so long ago. The possibility of the parachute failing to open and the prospect of meeting the ground with an unceremonious 'splat' failed to stir fear within me. I was more concerned about making sure I did not freak out or freeze when taking that plunge.

At seventeen, I was taking on something many adults would never consider. It took me right out of my comfort zone, as I had to relinquish control to another because I was to be doing a tandem dive. I liked control and being the one who was making the decisions and choices. This would be an experience where I let someone else take the lead and put my safety and life into their hands. This terrified me more than anything else, letting myself be vulnerable and allowing that trust in another.

We sat around for what seemed like an eternity but was probably not that long. I am not the most patient person in the world, and I hate waiting with nothing to do. Broken Hill Airport is not a substantial, bustling place. The hanger we were based out of to do the skydive was away from the main terminal, so there was not even a café or an area to wait in.

Gathered for the safety education session, we formed an eager yet apprehensive group as the instructors imparted the basics. The stark reality of skydiving's risks became more confronting at that moment – once you signed that waiver, it felt as though you were surrendering more than just your signature; you were, in a sense, entrusting your life to fate.

With the safety brief concluded, JR and I aimlessly wandered around, attempting to distract me from the impatience of waiting. As the minutes passed, I became increasingly excited about what lay ahead. Still, also, it was time for the nerves and anxiety to build, and I was an equal balance of scared and eager all at the same time. I was left unsure whether to embrace the impending thrill or succumb to the fluttering butterflies in my stomach.

Before I could let the weight of anticipation overwhelm me, my name was called, signalling that it was finally my turn. With my heart pounding in my chest, I made my way to the waiting plane, feeling a surge of adrenaline coursing through my veins.

Each harness strap felt like a lifeline, securing me for the exhilarating journey ahead. It definitely crossed my mind that there was a chance that the parachute was not packed properly, or something may not have gone to plan, but there was no time left for worry; everything was happening all at once, and it was not in my personality to chicken out and not go ahead with the exercise.

Accompanying me on this daring adventure was the instructor, who was my trusted tandem partner, and three other of his colleagues who had journeyed from Adelaide to share in the thrill. Two of them were equipped with cameras attached to their helmets, poised to capture every moment of our descent from a bird's eye view.

Amidst the flurry of excitement, a brief final explanation of the exit strategy was delivered, a last preparation before taking the plunge.

We climbed aboard, all squashing into the back of a tiny mail carrier plane. There was only the pilot seat up front and the cramped cargo area at the back, which now accommodated five people and all our gear. Despite the dubious appearance of the plane and the knowledge I had of light planes being at a high risk of crashing, I figured that at least we had parachutes if the aircraft were to suddenly fall out of the sky.

Squeezed tightly together, I couldn't shake the nagging worry of developing a dead leg or experiencing pins and needles from the confined space. Amidst the confined quarters, the air was filled with nervous laughter and casual banter, a feeble attempt to alleviate the tension within us all. Even though I was with a group of seasoned skydiving professionals, an element of risk and adrenaline flooded the plane.

As the aircraft ascended to our designated altitude of 10,000 feet, I stole a moment to peer out the window. Below, the vast expanse of Broken Hill stretched out in all directions. The red dirt contrasted with the clear blue sky.

Anticipation hung thick in the air, mingling with the engine's hum and the butterflies in my tummy. Suddenly, a strange silence descended at the drop spot as the engine either cut or stalled, leaving the aircraft eerily suspended in mid-air. It was time to exit.

The girls, equipped with their cameras, were the first to leap into the open sky, their figures suspended from the wing struts awaiting the queue to let go simultaneously. Soon, it was my turn. I was positioned on the wing alongside my instructor, ready to embrace the exhilarating plunge into the unknown.

The instructor initiated the countdown before I could fully comprehend what was happening. In a heartbeat, we were hurtling through the air. There was no time for hesitation or second-guessing; I was simply swept up in the moment's momentum. Attached to him, I surrendered to the directive to leap when he did, the decision made for me.

"*Woohoo!*" off the wing we dove. Flying free through the air. The wind rushed around me from all angles. The sky was so blue, and it felt like you could just reach out and touch a cloud.

The free fall was over before I thought about it. The girls with the camera got us to do a formation and took loads of footage as they flew past me. Waving my arms around like a bird was quite a thrill. We reached the point where the parachute needed to be pulled. I had been having so much fun that I did not even think about the parachute until then.

The instructor had advised that I could pull the strap for the parachute when he indicated so this one was on me. He gave me the signal, and I pulled the string, and bam! The parachute came out all as it was supposed to, and the rest of the flight was a gentle float to the ground.

We even did some tricky spins as we floated down. This felt like a bird, not flying through the air at a massive speed but peacefully gliding toward the ground with the breeze flowing all around.

As we calmly descended, I could look at the landscape and take it all in. I felt such tranquillity, enjoying the beauty of nature, even though I still had a flood of adrenaline pumping through my veins.

Underneath it all, Broken Hill is a beautiful place with such unique geology and natural beauty. I took a moment to really absorb what I was viewing and that the reason for the skydive competition entry was not just me being tricky and making my disability the reason for a good entry but realising that the reason was valid.

I was going to go blind, and the opportunity to take in the natural beauty of the place where I had grown up was something I needed to secure in the memory banks. It was something that I would never experience again. I knew I had a plan to leave Broken Hill after school finished, and who knew when I would be back and if I would ever see the place from that perspective with any usable vision ever again.

It was really like one of those landscape paintings from the outback. Blue sky with little fluffy white clouds, red dirt, and gum trees. Very much, iconically Broken Hill and the Australian outback. Harsh, but beautiful in its harshness.

Coming into land was like an anticlimax. It was like stepping off a big step from the sky onto the ground. We ended up right on the target outside the airport hangar that we had left half an hour before. JR and my family were there to greet me.

I was so hyped. The adrenaline ran for days. It was such a fantastic experience, and I just wanted more and more adventure. I had so much adrenaline and energy that I did not want to sit. I could have run a marathon. JR and I decided to go for a walk while we waited for the film footage to be ready. He asked me if doing the skydive had changed my life, as I had spoken about as part of the radio competition entry.

At that moment, a profound realisation washed over me. It wasn't just the thrill of adventure that had captivated me; it was the sense of freedom and independence that came with it. For the first time, I understood the beauty of relinquishing control, of allowing someone else – be it my instructor or the universe itself – to guide my path.

For so long, I had meticulously orchestrated every aspect of my life, ensuring everything fell into place according to plan. I had discovered a newfound liberation – a freedom that stemmed from surrendering to the unknown and embracing the uncertainty of letting go. It was a revelation that left me feeling empowered and alive.

The danger of plummeting from the sky had held little fear for me; my mortality seemed a distant concern, a concept I had grown accustomed to disregarding. Instead, it was the relinquishing of control, the surrender to the inexorable momentum of the dive, that stirred something within me – a flicker of apprehension and a tinge of uncertainty. An unasked question of whether I had the ability, maturity, and inner strength to take upon such a challenge.

For someone who had spent the better part of the past two years numb to the world, the sensation of fear mingled with exhilaration sparked something deep within me. It was as if the dormant emotions had been awoken, showing me I could experience fun and vitality. It was like a switch had been flicked, and my spirit had been reignited.

It was a revelation that left me feeling invincible, capable of conquering the skies and the challenges ahead in life's uncertain journey. If I could skydive, I could do anything I set my mind to.

By asking the most basic question, JR had made me understand for myself that I was able to see my inner power and that I could achieve what I wanted to. That I was strong and capable and that even though I had spent so much time telling myself I was worthless. This was not true.

I returned to school the following week with a renewed vigour to push myself and ensure that my dreams would become a reality. All of a sudden, what the others around me thought, the kids who were dismissive or cruel meant nothing, in the light of my newfound purpose.

Even the lingering sorrow of my father's absence and the challenges of navigating adolescence while grappling with the impending loss of my sight seemed to pale in comparison to the singular focus that now consumed me. Once I had this new knowledge and drive, it was like having blinkers on, and all the other things holding me back became inconsequential.

When I next encountered my legal studies teacher - the same one I had confided in about my struggles with suicidal thoughts the year before – he broached the subject of my recent skydiving adventure, his curiosity piqued by the newfound determination that seemed to radiate from within me.

In true teenage fashion, I declared it was the best day of my life and had heaps of fun. With a vulnerability that surprised even me, I added that it had literally changed my life and that I had realised that I needed to change my focus toward the future rather than what I had been doing, which was dwelling on things that were in the past or fixating on circumstances out of my control.

He seemed surprised at this revelation but promised to do all he could to support my endeavours. His response was one of unwavering support. Alongside the rest of the teaching staff, he steadfastly believed in my abilities, affirming a commitment to helping me achieve the academic success necessary for university admission.

I felt a surge of gratitude for the unwavering support of those who had never lost faith in my potential, even in my darkest hours. With the guidance and encouragement of the teaching staff, I knew that the path forward was paved with possibility and I was ready to embark on the journey toward a brighter future.

That skydive profoundly impacted my life – far beyond the thrill of experiencing the beauty of the world around me before I lost my sight.

If I could summon the courage to leap from a plane, an act others shied away from in fear, then what else was within my grasp?

The barriers that had once seemed insurmountable began to crumble before me, replaced by a newfound sense of possibility and empowerment. I could do all the things that others took for granted; I could go to university; I could get a job and have the future I wanted, that could be in the place I chose.

The only thing stopping me was my own sense of self-doubt and depression. It was time to stop listening to that voice in my head and the nay-sayers on the outside who had no faith that I would reach my dreams. The skydive opened my eyes to the world's beauty and opened my heart to the boundless possibilities that awaited me on the journey ahead.

Dream Big or...

So, here was the deal – I had to figure out if my dreams were just in my head or if they could actually become my reality. It was time to sit down and get serious about what I wanted to achieve and how I would do it. Sure, it was easy to say I wanted to move to Sydney, attend university, and live a typical life. But let's face it, there were a lot of factors to think about, some tough decisions to make, and some significant obstacles to tackle to make all of this work out. It was time to roll up my sleeves and get down to business.

As kids, we all have dreams about what we want to be when we grow up. Firefighter, nurse, or police officer. Me? I wanted to be an English cop. There was just one minor hiccup – I wasn't English. Maybe I'd watched one too many episodes of *The Bill*. And then reality struck – I knew I couldn't join the police force because there's no such thing as a blind policewoman.

Astronaut, race car driver, surgeon... The list of dream jobs that seemed out of reach kept growing. Even back then, I knew I had to choose a path that wouldn't rely on my vision, given that I would lose sight as I grew up. Driving was out of the question, so I had to find something that wouldn't risk my life or anyone else's.

I remember the moment vividly when I decided I would be a journalist. I was sure it was the perfect fit for me – I could type and loved to write; what else could I ask for?

I told everyone my plan. No one stopped me in my delusional dreams of the future by asking if this was realistic. It was not until I started considering the logical steps to follow that I realised my mistake. Then reality hit me hard at sixteen.

How was I, a blind person, supposed to chase down stories in the field?

Before the internet ruled the world, you had to be physically present to gather information. The harsh truth sunk in – being a journalist was not on the cards for me. It was a tough pill to swallow, realising how much my disability would shape my future. Life felt like an uphill battle; every step forward was met with resistance and pain. Losing my dream career added another heavy burden to the load already weighing down on my shoulders. Nothing seemed to come together, and no solutions were in sight.

I knew that having a career was my ticket out of Broken Hill. It was my way of breaking free from the family nest. Going to university and carving out my own path was only possible with a solid plan and a career goal in sight. Seeing my sisters venture out after school and create their own lives inspired me. I wanted that independence for myself, too. I didn't want to dwell on the challenges my disability might bring – I just wanted to chase my dreams and be like everyone else.

So, after chatting with Mr. Mason, my legal studies teacher, it hit me – maybe there was something to this whole 'using my experiences to assist others and then gaining the skills to make a difference' thing. I'd been collaborating with social workers from *Vision Australia* for a while now, and their support during trips to camps and our phone catchups got me thinking that becoming a social worker could be an excellent path for me. Plus, I had heard tales about homeless street kids in Kings Cross, and it touched my heart – helping out this group could be super meaningful for me.

I thought seriously about it when I was at my lowest point – escaping to the city seemed like the perfect solution, and I dreamt of heading straight to Kings Cross. But let's be honest, that was just a wild fantasy. A small-town girl like me wouldn't have stood a chance in the hustle and bustle of Kings Cross. I would have been an easy target with my innocence, like a beacon shining for anyone looking to take advantage. But hey, maybe as a social worker or youth worker I could provide some much-needed support to the group I connected with.

Those kids in Kings Cross must have faced way more severe challenges than mine. I didn't experience physical abuse, substance abuse, or the constant dangers that homeless youth often have to deal with. It's funny how we tend to think our own problems are the worst until reality hits us – reminding us that there are always people out there facing much tougher situations than we are.

Later, when I finally moved to Sydney, I jumped into doing some volunteer work for the *Vinnies Youth Project*. And let me tell you, it was an eye-opening experience! I quickly realised that I didn't have the same street smarts as these kids at just eighteen years old. I felt like I couldn't offer much in terms of support.

It hit me hard that I still needed to figure out a lot about myself before I could really help others dealing with tough stuff like homelessness, abuse, and dependency. Seeing these teens going through such serious struggles gave me a glimpse into the harsh realities some young people face.

While I'd gone through some rough patches, these kids were dealing with intense challenges. I learned that despite my hardships, I still had some control over my choices – unlike many of these kids whose options were stripped away. This experience made me realise that I needed to gain practical skills to make a difference in their lives. It was a harsh but valuable lesson that helped me understand myself better and set me on the path to being able to offer meaningful help to others in the future.

Back in Grade Twelve, in my pursuit of becoming a social worker, the dream of leaving Broken Hill transformed from fantasy to a resolute goal. The final year of high school was a whirlwind of dedication and grit. While others embraced the joys of youth, I delved into textbooks and study guides, unwavering in my quest for academic excellence.

A sense of seriousness enveloped me, driving me to utilise every weekend and school night to meticulously review schoolwork, delve into additional texts and complete practice assessments in preparation for year-end exams. Amidst the intense study sessions, I sought teacher feedback and supplementary materials and crammed my mind with knowledge beyond what seemed humanly possible.

We had study weeks before the exams when it was not compulsory to attend school. I was the nerd who still wore the school uniform to fit in and went and sat at the school library or in an empty classroom to continue my studies. I knew that if I were at home, my mother would inevitably find chores or other things for me to do and that I would not be able to dedicate the time to my studies, so school was a place to hide from the household chores and distractions.

As a student from a remote area and a person with a disability, I secured special allowances from my chosen universities for reduced marks for entry, ensuring I had all contingencies covered. I applied to universities in Sydney, Adelaide, and Melbourne, resolute in my determination to gain higher education. I had my heart set on living in Sydney and had never even been to Melbourne, but I was determined to leave Broken Hill and start my life following my dream, and nothing would stop me.

Unlike today, the exam results were delayed until the first week of January. I remember the day vividly, as it was pivotal in shaping my future. The anticipation leading up to that momentous day, a week before my eighteenth birthday, was a mix of nerves and excitement. I had a sleepless night before, wondering and worrying about all the possibilities and what that score meant for the rest of my life.

In Broken Hill, we had a tradition of meeting at the main post office before opening time to get our results. We would then share scores with everyone else and do all the comparisons. At this time, I knew my vision was bad enough that I would need to read the results with a magnifier.

I was not going to whip out the magnifier like Sherlock Holmes in front of everyone else, so I decided to wait and walk down to the post office to get the results just before the cut off, where the postman would do it as a delivery. I went in and gave my name and got the envelope. I quickly stuffed it in my backpack and made my way out of the post office as soon as possible, avoiding any other school comrades who had left it at the exact moment to retrieve their results.

That envelope in my bag burned such a hole of curiosity in me all the way home. I had never hiked up the hill as fast as I did that day. Nervous but full of anticipation, I arrived home and emptied the contents of the magical envelope out onto the kitchen table. I did not need my magnifier to read the one key result I needed. That score out of 100 was the key to university entry and it was written in large print in the middle of the page....

I did it!

All the hard work had paid off, and I knew at that moment that I had choices, and my future was in my control. I have kept those papers to this day. The result would be the catalyst to open doors for the rest of my life. It was not an exceptional mark, nothing like my big sister had achieved, but it was what I needed to get me to the places I wanted to go and that was the most important thing.

My final results were enough to get me into any of the courses I had applied for. I did not need the additional special considerations offered to assist with the entry; I had the option of my first university choice in each state I had applied for. Which, of course, meant that I was off to Sydney to live my dream.

I called JR, Peter, and Kirsty. We all checked and compared our results to each other. I know that each had a plan for the following year, and their marks were not as important to them as mine were to me in relation to taking the next step in life. It was the end of an era and we all knew that our plans for the future would take us in different directions.

That night, I joined Peter, and we went to the local pub where we celebrated the outcomes of our high school results. I should not have gone as I was still one week short of being legally allowed to enter the premises, but it was the final time I would ever see and spend time with the people I had shared the school years with.

Some of them I had known since primary school; this was our last hoorah before we all went on different life journeys. I found Paul, with whom I had shared my night-time legal studies class, who had often given me a ride home. He and I had been the biggest competition for each other in the race for results. We had an unspoken rivalry between us as friendly competition. We had shared all but one class together, and I wanted to know his final results.

He was delighted to have got two marks more than me. We laughed and realised we could finally relax and stop trying to prove ourselves. He bought me a drink and joined the rest of our class of 1994 to celebrate a job well done.

In Sydney the following week – other than celebrating my eighteenth birthday with Renee and her family and our friends, enjoying the course at *Vision Australia* and revelling in the fact that I had finished school – I realised that I needed to start making some serious plans as to how I was going to make my move to Sydney work out.

The university I had been accepted into did not offer an on-campus living option. My brother had offered for me to stay with him and his family for a week or two while I got myself sorted out, but the prospect of what lay ahead of me suddenly dawned to be a serious undertaking. I knew I had the support of my friends in Sydney from the blind camps and that Renee and her family would look out for me, but I also knew that I had to get a plan of action soon.

I could not do much from Broken Hill, so after returning from Sydney from the course, I had a week of packing and saying my goodbyes to my friends and, one afternoon, boarded the Indian Pacific train to head to Sydney to start my new life.

My mother and sister came to the train station to see me off, and JR came along. There were tears, some of sadness, as I knew he was off to Norway for a year, and we would not see each other for a while. There were tears for what I was leaving behind, but there was also excitement about what lay ahead.

It was a very different experience getting on the train with my suitcase and other belongings all packed up at home, ready to send on in freight when I found a place to live. I was prepared to let the adventure begin but was sad to leave the place I had so much connection to that had been built over my childhood years. It had certainly not always been happy, but it was all I knew, and now I was about to go somewhere different and have to learn many new things.

Finding my own space in a bustling city, I savoured the freedom and independence that came with it. Adjusting to a new routine and nurturing friendships helped alleviate the initial loneliness.

Reflecting on my past in Broken Hill, I realised the significance of those formative years in shaping my identity and the importance of embracing change and growth.

I now needed to embrace that change and begin my new life, and the first step was finding myself a place to live. The university had a noticeboard with advertised accommodation options. I found a notice from a local physiotherapist who offered the back half of her house used as her practice premises to rent to students. The rent was manageable and meant I would have my own space rather than having to share with someone I did not know.

I was so excited. It was close to the university campus and an easy walk to the train station. I knew a few people who lived in the vicinity, and one of my best friends was only ten minutes away.

My new home. How exciting. Now, I needed to get my stuff sent from Broken Hill and get some things for the house. I was fortunate to have an insurance claim mature when I turned eighteen.

I had been in a car accident when I was young, and the insurance had been put in trust. This financial win fall allowed me to pay for all the things that I needed to set myself up in my new house. I was helped out by having a payment from the government due to my disability, but the lump sum from the insurance was the only reason that I was able to establish myself in my own home.

My parents were never in a position to help with university fees and living costs. I had seen my middle sister go through the drama she had when her finances prevented her from completing her university course; I swore this would not happen to me and I would be independent from the start.

I loved living in my own space. It was the best thing to listen to my music as loudly as I wanted, shower at 3am if I wished to, and have friends come over to my house to hang out.

When I first moved to Sydney, I felt lonely as I tried to settle in. I quickly realised that establishing a routine and keeping myself occupied was essential to combat the feelings of loneliness.

Every Wednesday, I would have dinner with a friend after university, and on Thursdays, I would go late-night shopping with another friend. Although we rarely made any purchases during our shopping trips, those moments were priceless because they strengthened our bond. Looking back, I understand that my friend recognised the importance of getting me out of the house and engaging with others, even if it was just through window shopping. His subtle gestures and thoughtful actions have impacted my life, shaping my experiences in ways that weren't immediately obvious at the time.

Broken Hill was such a distant part of my life. During that first year when Peter and JR were both overseas, I made sure to keep in touch with Kirsty and my old school friends as much as possible.

When I eventually returned for my university holidays in the middle of the year, I was convinced I had transformed into this cool city girl. It was a surreal feeling seeing familiar faces around town, classmates from my past, while proudly displaying my new mobile phone attached to my belt for all to see – it was the trend back then. Clad in stylish clothes and exuding a newfound confidence, I realised something profound.

The urge to compare myself to those who stayed in Broken Hill and prove how much better my life had become was futile.

I understood that the life I led and the person I became were my choices. It was up to me to leave behind the negative memories of Broken Hill and forge my own path. This town was no longer my home, and while it played a part in shaping me, it did not dictate my future self.

I don't often find myself returning to Broken Hill these days because most of my family has moved away from there. It's a place that holds memories of my past – a place where my choices can either celebrate or dismiss those memories. My sister followed her dreams and ventured even further abroad to Japan after I left Broken Hill.

As I reflect on my past in writing this book, I realise that many of my behaviours stem from my teenage years. I need to acknowledge this without letting it overshadow the good memories. Despite any unpleasant or negative experiences, plenty of fun times spent with family and friends have shaped who I am today.

Some of the friendships I formed in the past still hold strong today, reminding me of the lasting impact those relationships have had on my life.

Peter and Kirsty are still in my life. I also keep in touch with Renee, Karen, and others from blind camps. Shane, my Thursday night shopping buddy, is still my best mate, and our bond grows stronger with each passing year.

The poignant absence of JR is a reminder of memories past, prompting me to use only his initials in this book. While our paths have diverged for now, hope glimmers in the possibility of our reunion someday. Who knows what the future holds? Perhaps we will cross paths once more.

My story was not always happy, but to be where I am today, I needed to live through and learn all the lessons that have been presented to me.

As a parent now, I have tried parenting in a way I would have liked when I was younger. I still struggle with my mental health at times, but now know the warning signs and know the things that I can do to bring myself out of those thought patterns before they become a problem.

I still love adventure and will often take on challenges that push me outside my comfort zone just to prove that I can do it and that those experiences create a healthy level of fear in me and also make me grow.

I have used some adult wisdom to mend my relationship with my mother. To understand that she was doing what she had the resources to do at the time, and even though it was far from helpful, I had the opportunity to experience much more parental flexibility than my siblings.

Teenage years are often the toughest of your life, a time to experiment and to work out your identity. Also, it is a time that has added pressure from social expectations and to decide on a future you want to pursue.

Even though my teen years had a lot of lessons to learn and a lot of self-development for me, I know that I was lucky to have the resources that I did. Even though I had plenty of nay-sayers and people ready to bully me or put me down, I had a select group of people around who showed me friendship, love, and support.

I was given opportunities by adults such as my teachers and Renee's parents to step in and help where they could. Most of all, I had a spirit of persistence that my father instilled in me.

If I think about someone resilient and persistent in the face of adversity, it was him.

I send a silent thank you to the man who is no longer with us but shaped me more than anyone I am today. I have lived two-thirds of my life without him now, taken from me before I had a chance to learn as much as I wish, but I know in my heart that I am who I am because of what he taught me in those formative years.

Also no longer with us is Mr. Mason, my legal studies teacher who helped shape my life after Dad was no longer around to give me advice and guidance. I thank his daughter, who was one of my high school classmates, for sharing her father with me – unknowingly at the time – as his words and impact changed my path in life.

Those years were not my most emotionally difficult; that is a story for another book, but they are full of growth and unveil my future identity. There were times when I wanted to escape and let the darkness take me away from my pain; I now realise that darkness is always a contrast to the light that shines in the happy moments.

The light that appears when I think of some of those times shared with my dad, big sister or my friends in the past that were truly happy. I have taken away an abundance of self-understanding from writing this all down, knowing that there are still gaps in my memory but that I have now created something that I can leave as a legacy for my children.

And as fate would have it, my youngest daughter graduated high school this week, so the timing couldn't be better. My reflections of my stories and past are something that I can now share with my daughters and the world, without fear or uncertainty, and I have the chance to thank and acknowledge those who had such a powerful impact.

Finally, as I look back on my journey so far, I realise that I am not, and have never been, *Broken*. I've just been climbing a rather rocky *Hill*.

About The Author

Fiona Demark's inspiring journey highlights the remarkable power of resilience and a can-do attitude. As an inspirational speaker and resilience coach, Fiona leads with authenticity, sharing her extraordinary story of conquering adversity and achieving success despite being legally blind since birth. Through her optimism and drive, Fiona empowers those feeling stuck and frustrated to rewrite their own narratives.

Drawing from a background in social work, accessibility and inclusion, Fiona skilfully combines her diverse talents to guide individuals through significant life transitions. Her extensive experience working with a varied clientele – delivering impactful messages to corporate audiences, uncovering unique talents, and managing her own business – exemplifies her unwavering dedication to supporting others on their journeys.

Despite her visual impairment, Fiona embraces life wholeheartedly through her heightened senses, finding joy in the simplest pleasures like the scent of rain, the warmth of the sun and the flavour of a delicious meal. Her adventurous spirit, refusal to back down from challenges and passion for sharing her story with diverse audiences make her a truly captivating role model.

Fiona's ultimate mission is to raise awareness, cultivate connections and guide others through their own trials. Through speaking engagements, coaching sessions, and personalised support, she embodies the belief that embracing one's identity – including its obstacles – can lead to genuine success and fulfilment.

Book Fiona for your next event to be inspired and empowered with practical tools, and challenged to embrace personal change:

www.fionademark.com.au

www.facebook.com/Fiona.Demark/

www.instagram.com/blind_inspirational_speaker/

www.linkedin.com/in/fionademark/

www.tiktok.com/@fiona.demark

www.youtube.com/@fionademarkblindinspiratio7752

Notes

www.ingramcontent.com/pod-product-compliance
Lightning Source LLC
Chambersburg PA
CBHW030038100526
44590CB00011B/256